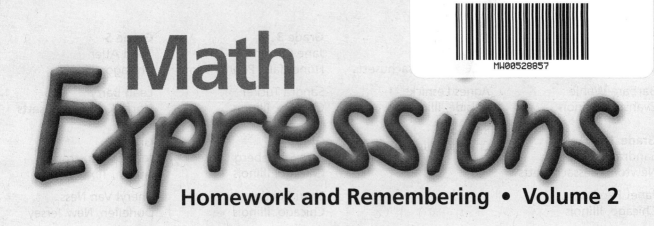

Math Expressions

Homework and Remembering • Volume 2

Dr. Karen C. Fuson
and
Dr. Sybilla Beckmann

This material is based upon work supported by the
National Science Foundation
under Grant Numbers
ESI-9816320, REC-9806020, and RED-935373.

Any opinions, findings, and conclusions, or recommendations expressed in this material
are those of the author and do not necessarily reflect the views of the National Science Foundation.

HOUGHTON MIFFLIN HARCOURT

Teacher Reviewers

Credits

Cover art: (wolf) Lynn Rogers/Photolibrary; (branches) Matthias Bein/dpa/Corbis

Homework

1. Circle the expressions.

$3 \cdot x = 9$ $3 \cdot x + 9$ 13 $r = s + t$ $5 \cdot (m + 4)$ $36 \div f + 17$

2. Write an expression that consists of three terms.

_____

3. Write an expression that consists of two terms that are numbers.

_____

Simplify each expression by following the Order of Operations.

4. $18 - 12 \div 3$ _____

5. $4 \cdot (7 + 5)$ _____

6. $7 \cdot 5 + 5 \cdot 7$ _____

7. $6 \cdot (21 \div 7) + 12$ _____

8. $36 \div 3 \cdot 2$ _____

9. $(5 + 2) \cdot 6 \div 7$ _____

Order of Operations

1. Perform all operations inside parentheses.

2. Multiply and divide from left to right.

3. Add and subtract from left to right.

Evaluate each expression for $a = 4$ and $b = 5$.

10. $60 - 16 \div a$ _____

11. $2 + 6 \cdot b$ _____

12. $a \cdot (b + 5)$ _____

13. $b + (4 - a) \cdot 9$ _____

Remembering

1. Maria is knitting a scarf. So far the scarf has 21 rows of white and 27 rows of red. She continues to knit more rows in the same basic ratio. How many rows of red will the scarf have when it has 42 rows of white?

_____

Solve.

2. $3.4 \cdot 0.21$ **3.** $233.1 \div 2.1$ **4.** $1,030 - 886$ **5.** $22.34 + 9.322$

_____   _____   _____   _____

The base of each three-dimensional figure is a regular polygon. Name the figure. Then find the surface area.

6.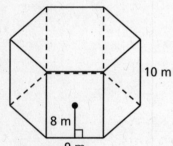

7.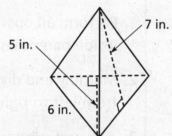

8.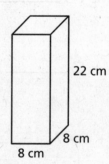

_____   _____   _____

9. **Stretch Your Thinking** How can you place parentheses in the expression below to make it have a value 60? Explain.

$$2 \cdot 6 + 6 + 3 \cdot 2$$

_____

_____

_____

_____

Expressions and Order of Operations

Homework

Write each expression as a repeated multiplication.

1. $7^3 =$ _____

2. $9^3 \cdot 2^2 =$ _____

3. $v^4 =$ _____

4. $a^4 \cdot b^2 =$ _____

Use an exponent to write each repeated multiplication.

5. $6 \cdot 6 \cdot 6 \cdot 6 \cdot 6 =$ _____

6. $n \cdot n \cdot n =$ _____

7. $4 \cdot t \cdot t =$ _____

8. $d \cdot d \cdot d \cdot f =$ _____

Simplify. Follow the Order of Operations.

9. $30 - 4^2 =$ _____

10. $(6 + 2) \div 2^2 =$ _____

11. $3^3 \div 9 + 3 =$ _____

Evaluate the expression for $a = 2$ and $b = 5$.

12. $6 \cdot a^3$ _____

13. $b^2 \cdot (a + 3)$ _____

14. $(b + a)^2$ _____

15. Match the terms of the expression to parts of the figure.

$3^2 + 2^2$ dots

16. Match the terms of the expression to parts of the figure.

$5^2 - 2^2$ dots

17. Riley said that $4^5 = 20$. What mistake did Riley make? What does 4^5 mean?

_____

_____

Remembering

1. At soccer practice, for every 5 minutes that Bob runs, he spends 20 minutes practicing dribbling. If Bob keeps the same ratio and he spends 36 minutes practicing dribbling, how many minutes does he spend running?

_____

2. Barb is making a banner that is shaped like a trapezoid. The height of the banner is 24 inches. The top of the banner is 14 inches. If the area of the banner is 372 in.^{2}, what is the length of the bottom side?

_____

3. Stephen is covering a box with felt. The box is in the shape of a rectangular prism. The height is 12 in. The length and width of the base are 5 in. and 6 in. How much felt does Stephen need to completely cover the box?

Simplify each expression by following the order of operations.

4. $22 - 5 \cdot 3$ _____

5. $6 \cdot (5 + 12)$ _____

6. $16 + 45 \div 9$ _____

7. $5 \cdot 6 + 3 \cdot 4$ _____

Evaluate each expression for $n = 5$ and $m = 3$.

8. $m + 4 \cdot 7$ _____

9. $30 - n \cdot 4 + m$ _____

10. $7 + n \cdot m \div 5$ _____

11. $n + (7 - m) \cdot 8$ _____

12. **Stretch Your Thinking** Justine evaluated this expression for a certain value of s and got 13. What was the value of s? Explain.

$$15 + s \div 3 - 6$$

_____

_____

Expressions with Exponents

Complete the table.

	Algebraic Expression	Plus, Minus, Times, Divided by	Add, Subtract, Multiply, Divide	Sum, Difference, Product, Quotient
1.	_____	___ minus ___	Subtract d from 11.	_____ is a _____.
2.	$7 \cdot d$	7 _____ d	Multiply ___ and ___.	_____ is the _____ of ___ and ___.
3.	$7 \div d$	___ divided by ___	Divide ___ by ___.	_____ is a _____.

Analyze the expression. Then match the expression with the diagram that describes it.

4. $5 \cdot n^2 - 3$ ____   5. $3 \cdot n - 6 \div 5^2$ ____   6. $(3 + n) \cdot 5 + n^2$ ____

A.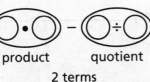

B.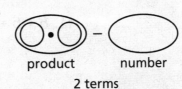

C.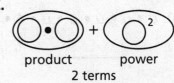

Analyze each expression. Then make a diagram to describe it.

7. $6 \cdot 7 + c$ 8. $6 \cdot (7 + c)$ 9. $c \div 7 - 6 \cdot c$

10. Evaluate $\frac{1}{2} \cdot a + 1$ for $a = 9$.

_____

Name ___ **Date** ___

Remembering

Write equivalent fractions. Complete.

1.	$5\frac{2}{3}$ $3\frac{7}{10}$ →	
2.	>, <	
3.	+	
4.	−	
5.	•	
6.	÷	

Solve.

7. At *Buy It Here*, Katie can buy 4 cans of soup for $10. At *SuperMarket*, she can buy 18 cans of soup for $30. Katie wants to buy soup for the lowest possible price. At which store should she shop? Explain.

_____

_____

_____

Write each expression as a repeated multiplication or with an exponent.

8. $5 \cdot r \cdot r \cdot r$ _____

9. 5^4v _____

10. $u \cdot u \cdot u \cdot u \cdot u \cdot 4 \cdot 4$ _____

11. $b \cdot b \cdot y \cdot y \cdot y$ _____

Evaluate each expression for $p = 4$ and $q = 7$.

12. $2 \cdot p^2$ _____

13. $(p + q)^2$ _____

14. $2^3 \cdot p^2 \div 2$ _____

15. $q^2 - (p \cdot 5)$ _____

16. **Stretch Your Thinking** Maryanna drew this figure. Write an expression that represents the number of dots. Explain.

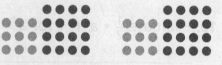

_____

_____

_____

Interpreting and Analyzing Expressions

Homework

1. Analyze the expression. Then match parts of the expression with parts of the dot design.

   $4 + 3 \cdot 5$

2. Analyze the expression. Then evaluate it for $d = 7$.

   $4 + 3 \cdot d$ _____

3. Analyze and simplify each expression. Put checkmarks next to the expressions with the same value.

   $2 + 4 \cdot 3$ _____ $2 + (4 \cdot 3)$ _____ $(2 + 4) \cdot 3$ _____

Write each word expression as an algebraic expression.

4. the product of $\frac{1}{3}$ and a _____

5. Divide a by 3. _____

6. Subtract $\frac{1}{3}$ from b. _____

Write an expression for the number of dots. Then analyze the expression and evaluate or simplify it.

7.

   Write an expression and analyze it.

   _____

   Evaluate the expression for $m = 5$.

   _____

8.

   Write an expression and analyze it.

   _____

   Simplify the expression.

   _____

Analyze the expression. Then draw a diagram for the expression.

9. $4 \cdot 6 - 3$

10. $3 \cdot (2 + 5) + 4$

Name _____ **Date** _____

Remembering

1. For a field trip, 4 chaperones are needed for every 18 students. How many chaperones are needed if there are 81 students going on the trip?

   _____

2. The base of a prism is a regular hexagon with a perimeter of 78 mm. The height of the prism is 16 mm. What is the area of one of the rectangular faces of the prism?

   _____

Solve.

3. $\frac{6}{7} + \frac{1}{2}$

   _____

4. $5.6 \cdot 0.21$

   _____

5. $3.012 \div 6$

   _____

6. $\frac{1}{3} \cdot \frac{2}{3}$

   _____

7. $1{,}330 + 2{,}391$

   _____

8. $\frac{3}{5} - \frac{1}{4}$

   _____

9. $67 \div 12$

   _____

10. $2\frac{1}{5} - 1\frac{3}{8}$

    _____

Evaluate each expression for $h = 2$ and $r = 3$.

11. $4 \cdot h^2 + r$ _____

12. $r + 16 \div 2 + h$ _____

13. $h \cdot (6 + r)^2$ _____

14. $h \cdot (r - 1) \cdot 12$ _____

Write an expression for each phrase.

15. subtract 6 from y _____

16. the product of 8 and g _____

17. divide 45 by x _____

18. the sum of 15 and d _____

19. **Stretch Your Thinking** Jackie evaluated these expressions for a value for c and got the same number. What could be the value of c? Explain.

$$40 - c^2 \cdot 7 + 2 \cdot c$$
$$\text{and}$$
$$40 - 2 \cdot c \cdot 7 + c^2$$

_____

_____

_____

Modeling and Simplifying Expressions

Homework

Consider the floor plan shown at the right.
(All the angles are right angles.)

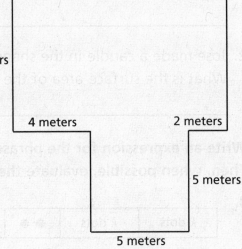

1. One expression for the area is given below.
   Analyze the expression and explain how it
   relates to the drawing.

   $12 \cdot 11 - 4 \cdot 5 - 2 \cdot 5 \ m^2$

   _____

   _____

   _____

2. Write a different expression for the area.

   _____

3. Explain how your expression from Exercise 2 relates
   to the drawing.

   _____

   _____

At the right is the net for a cube with edges of length e cm.
One expression for the surface area of the cube is $6 \cdot e^2$.

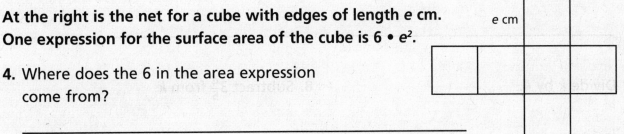

4. Where does the 6 in the area expression
   come from?

   _____

5. Where does the e^2 come from?

   _____

6. Write another expression for the surface area of the cube.

   _____

7. How much paper would it take to cover a cube with edges
   2.5 centimeters long?

   _____

Remembering

1. Matt saves the same amount each week. At the end of 3 weeks, he has $12. How many weeks will it take him to save $36?

   _____

2. Jose made a candle in the shape shown. What is the surface area of the candle?

   _____

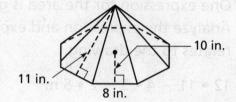

10 in.

11 in.

8 in.

Write an expression for the phrase or number of dots.
Then, when possible, evaluate the expression for $k = 12$.

3.

| k dots | k dots | ●● | ●● |

_____

4.

_____

5.

_____

6.

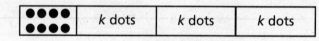

| ●●●● ●●●● | k dots | k dots | k dots |

_____

7. Divide k by 4.

   _____

8. Subtract $3\frac{4}{5}$ from k.

   _____

9. **Stretch Your Thinking** Make a diagram for the expression $4 \cdot (n + 4)$. Explain how your diagram shows the expression.

   _____

   _____

   _____

Expressions for Area and Surface Area

Homework

Write two expressions that are equivalent to each expression.

1. $3f$ _____

2. $4 \cdot g$ _____

3. $h + h$ _____

4. Describe a situation and make a diagram
   for the expression $2a + a$.

   Situation   **Diagram**

   _____

   _____

   _____

   _____

5. Circle the expressions that are equivalent to $2a + a$.

   $2 \cdot a + 1 \cdot a$ $a + a + a$ $a + 2a$ $3a$ $2 + 2a$

6. Circle the expressions that are equivalent to $4b - 4$.

   $4 \cdot b - 4$ $(4 \cdot b) - 4$ b $b + b + b + b - 4$ $(4 + b) - 4$

7. Make a diagram and write an equivalent expression
   for $1 + 2 + h$.

   Diagram   **Expression**

Remembering

1. June and her brother Jason both read for the same amount of time at their own constant rates. When June has read 35 pages, Jason has read 42 pages. How many pages will June have read when Jason has read 48 pages?

_____

Evaluate each expression for $a = 3$ and $b = 4$.

2. $5 \cdot b^2 + (2 \cdot a + 2)$ _____

3. $(b + a)^2 - 12 + a$ _____

4. $64 \div b \cdot a$ _____

5. $a^2 - b + 5 \cdot a$ _____

6. Write two expressions to find the area of the figure at the right. Then use the expressions to find the area.

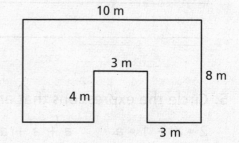

_____

7. Write two expressions to find the surface area of the figure at the right. Then use the expressions to find the surface area.

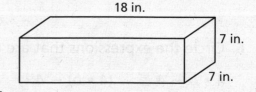

_____

8. **Stretch Your Thinking** Write an expression to show the surface area of a rectangular prism with length, *l*, width, *w*, and height, *h*. Now double the dimensions of the prism. Write a new expression to show the surface area of the larger prism. Explain how your expressions show the measurements.

_____

_____

_____

_____

Name _____ **Date** _____

Homework

1. Use the diagram to help you combine like terms and find an equivalent expression that is simpler.

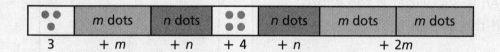

| :: | m dots | n dots | :: | n dots | m dots | m dots |
| 3 | + m | + n | + 4 | + n | + 2m | |

$3 + m + n + 4 + n + 2m =$ _____

Simplify each expression by combining like terms.

2. $4x + 5 + x + 3 =$ _____

3. $2a + 2b + 3a + 5 - b - 3 =$ _____

4. $10 + 4y + 5 + 6y =$ _____

5. $6 + 8x + 5y + 2 + x =$ _____

6. $4 + w^2 + 5 + w^2 =$ _____

7. $3c^2 + 1 + c^2 =$ _____

Rewrite the term so the coefficient is in front.

8. $(3x)8 =$ _____

coefficient: _____

9. $(4y)2y =$ _____

coefficient: _____

10. $(4p)(3q) =$ _____

coefficient: _____

11. There are 10 boxes. Each box has 4 six-packs of juice. Each six-pack has 6 bottles.

Explain why the expression $(10 \cdot 4) \cdot 6$ represents the total number of bottles of juice.

_____

_____

Simplify $(10 \cdot 4) \cdot 6$. _____

Explain why the expression $10 \cdot (4 \cdot 6)$ represents the total number of bottles of juice.

_____

_____

Simplify $10 \cdot (4 \cdot 6)$ _____

Remembering

Solve.

Write equivalent fractions. Complete.

1. The ratio of width to length of Baily's television screen is 3:4. What is the width of the screen if the length is 32 inches?

_____

3.	$5\frac{3}{8}$ $4\frac{3}{4}$	→	
4.	>, <	
5.	+	
6.	−	
7.	•	
8.	÷	

2. Erin is painting a block the shape of a square pyramid. The length of one side of the base of the pyramid is 8 in. The height of one of the triangular sides of the pyramid is 12.3 in. How much area does Erin need to cover with paint?

_____

Write two expressions that are equivalent to each expression.

9. $5t$ _____

10. $k + k + k$ _____

11. $y + y + y + y - 4$ _____

12. $10 + 3 \cdot d$ _____

13. Circle the expressions that are equivalent to $3r - 3$.

$2r$ $r + r + r - 3$ r $(3 \cdot r) - 3$ $2r + r - 3$

14. **Stretch Your Thinking** Decide if the expressions $4 + (5 \cdot t)$ and $2 + 2 + t + t + 3t$ are equivalent. Then find the value of each expression if $t = 3$. Explain your results.

_____

_____

_____

_____

_____

The Commutative and Associative Properties

Use the Distributive Property to write an equivalent expression.

1. $x(x + 3) =$ _____

2. $4y + 7y =$ _____

3. $(y - 2)x =$ _____

4. $12(x + 5) =$ _____

5. $3x - 6 =$ _____

6. $(4x - 1)x =$ _____

7. $y \cdot 3 + z \cdot 3 =$ _____

8. $xy + xz =$ _____

Write each sum as a product by using the Distributive Property to pull out the greatest common factor. Show all your steps.

Example: $56 + 63 = 7 \cdot 8 + 7 \cdot 9 = 7(8 + 9) = 7 \cdot 17$

9. $48 + 42 =$ _____ • _____ + _____ • _____ = _____ = _____

10. $35 + 15 =$ _____ • _____ + _____ • _____ = _____ = _____

Tell whether the expressions are equivalent.

11. $4(xy)$ and $(4x)(4y)$ _____

12. $9 + 2(x + y)$ and $9 + 2x + 2y$ _____

13. $2 + 2m + 3$ and $2m + 5$ _____

14. $2 + 2m + 3$ and $2(1 + m) + 3$ _____

15. $2 + 2m + 3$ and $4m + 3$ _____

16. $(4 + x) + (4 + y)$ and $4(x + y)$ _____

Rewrite the term so the coefficient is in front.

17. $(2x)5x =$ _____

coefficient: _____

18. $(3y)2 =$ _____

coefficient: _____

19. $(6j)(5k) =$ _____

coefficient: _____

Name _____ **Date** _____

Remembering

1. Kendra is buying notebooks for school. The table shows 4 different notebooks and their prices. If Kendra wants to buy 16 notebooks at the least expensive price, which notebook should she buy?

   _____

Cost of Notebooks	
Notebook A	4 for $6
Notebook B	16 for $24
Notebook C	8 for $10
Notebook D	1 for $5

2. Mario is covering the room shown at the right with carpeting. Write an expression that can be used to find the amount of carpeting he needs. Then use the expression to find the amount of carpeting he needs.

   _____

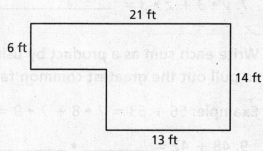

Simplify each expression by combining like terms.

3. $6x + 10 - x + 9$

   _____

4. $10 + 5f + 6 + 2f - 9$

   _____

5. $m^2 + 12 + 3m^2 + 5n + 3 - n$

   _____

6. $3w + 4u + 9 + 2w + 5u + 1$

   _____

Rewrite the term so the coefficient is in front.

7. $(9r)2$ _____

8. $8e(7e)t$ _____

9. $(3p)(8s)$ _____

10. **Stretch Your Thinking** The diagram shows $4 \cdot (m \cdot 3)$. Change the diagram so that it shows $(4 \cdot m) \cdot 3$. How do the diagrams show that $4 \cdot (m \cdot 3) = (4 \cdot m) \cdot 3 = 12m$?

m dots	m dots	m dots	m dots
m dots	m dots	m dots	m dots
m dots	m dots	m dots	m dots

   _____

   _____

   _____

   _____

The Distributive Property

Homework

1. Ms. Williams brought 7 boxes of m markers to school. At the end of the school day 3 markers were missing.

   Write an expression for the number of markers that were left.

   _____

   Evaluate your expression for $m = 12$.

   _____ markers

Apply the Distributive Property to write an equivalent expression.

2. $6s - 42 =$ _____

3. $9(t + 8) =$ _____

4. $5p + 2p =$ _____

5. $m(3 - m) =$ _____

Tell whether the expressions are equivalent.

6. $(4a)(4b)$ and $16ab$ _____

7. $2m + 2 + 3m$ and $5m + 2$ _____

8. $4 + 7(x + y)$ and $4 + 7x + y$ _____

9. $4x^2$ and $(2x)(2x)$ _____

Simplify each expression. Be sure to do the following:

- **Do all the computations you can.**

- **Write each term with the coefficient in front.**

- **Combine like terms.**

10. $2^2 + x + 3^2 + x =$ _____

11. $5a + 5b + 2a + 3b =$ _____

12. $4 \cdot 5 + 3(2x) + 5x + 3 =$ _____

13. $(5m)5 + 2m + 5(6m) =$ _____

Name _____ **Date** _____

Remembering

1. Michelle and Matthew bake carrot cake at their bakery. For every 9 cups of shredded carrots they use, they use 6 cups of sugar. How many cups of shredded carrots will they use if they use 14 cups of sugar?

_____

Solve.

2. $15 \cdot 3.4$

_____

3. $2,444 + 703$

_____

4. $105.84 \div 2.4$

_____

5. $2.031 + 0.978$

_____

6. $1.12 \cdot 0.3$

_____

7. $3,024 \div 56$

_____

8. $9.1 - 1.02$

_____

9. $48.45 \div 9.5$

_____

Tell if the expressions are equivalent.

10. $2x + 3x + 7$ and $6x^2 + 7$ _____

11. $4 + 4u + 8$ and $4(1 + u + 2)$ _____

12. $4m - 4 + 3$ and $4(m - 1) + 3$ _____

13. $(5 + b) + (5 + g)$ and $5(b + g)$ _____

Use the Distributive Property to write an equivalent expression.

14. $y(u + 7)$ _____

15. $24 + 12s + 12r$ _____

16. $5t + 6t + tm$ _____

17. $7(u + 4 + h)$ _____

18. **Stretch Your Thinking** Explain how you can use the Distributive Property to find $25 \cdot 43$.

_____

_____

_____

_____

Practice with Expressions

Homework

**Maria and Juan are sister and brother. Maria is
2 years older than Juan.**

1. Define the variables for Maria's and Juan's ages.

   Let m be _____

   Let j be _____

2. Fill in the table, make a diagram, and
   write equations to relate m and j.

Table		Diagram	Equations

Table

j	m

Diagram

Equations

$m = $ _____

$j = $ _____

Write the expression that matches the description.

3. Subtract x from 4. _____

4. Multiply 3 times p and then add 10 to the result. _____

5. Divide 12 by the sum of x and 9. _____

6. Subtract 7 from s and then multiply the result by 6. _____

**Apply the Distributive Property to all or part of the
expression to write an equivalent expression.**

7. $d(d - 1) = $ _____   8. $15x + 10 = $ _____

9. $(6m - 7)6 = $ _____   10. $4(a + 3) + c = $ _____

11. $3 + 7y + 5y = $ _____   12. $2x + 3x^2 = $ _____

Remembering

1. Benny is writing a report. For every 7 paragraphs, he uses 4 pieces of art. How many pieces of art will Benny use if his report is 56 paragraphs long?

   _____

2. On the grid at the right, plot these ordered pairs: $A(1, 2)$, $B(9, 2)$, $C(14, 14)$. Plot point D and draw lines to form parallelogram $ABCD$. Segment AD is 13 units long. Find the perimeter and area of parallelogram $ABCD$.

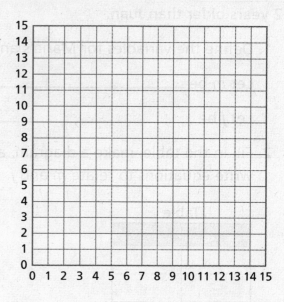

   $P =$ _____

   $A =$ _____

Evaluate the expression for $n = 4$ and $t = 2$.

3. $6n + 16 + t \cdot (2 + n)$ _____

4. $n \cdot (5 + 12) - n^2 + t$ _____

5. $6 + n^2 \cdot 7 - 12 \div t$ _____

6. $t + 48 \div 4 - n \cdot t$ _____

Simplify each expression.

7. $v + 3^2 + 3v - 4$

8. $5b + 7a + 15 - a + 2b - 10$

   _____

9. $4m(8) + 4m + 16 \cdot 2 - 3m$

10. $7(2j + 5) - 12 + 6j$

   _____   _____

11. **Stretch Your Thinking** Malia used the Distributive Property when she simplified an expression. The simplified expression was $4 + 3a + 17m$. What could have been the original expression? Explain.

   _____

   _____

   _____

Relating Two Quantities

Name _____ **Date** _____

Homework

A student walks at a constant rate of 9 feet every 2 seconds.

1. Label a double number line for the student.

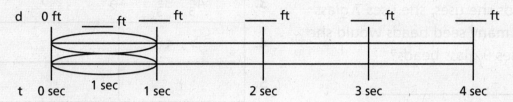

d   0 ft   ____ ft   ____ ft   ____ ft   ____ ft

t   0 sec   1 sec   1 sec   2 sec   3 sec   4 sec

2. Complete the table for the student's walk.

Seconds Elapsed	Feet Walked
0	
1	
2	
3	
4	
5	
t	d

3. Graph the data from the table. Draw two unit rate triangles on the graph.

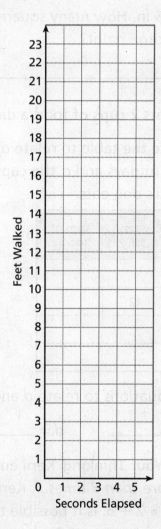

Feet Walked / Seconds Elapsed

4. Write an equation relating seconds elapsed t and feet walked d.

_____

Tell how far the student walks in the given amount of time.

5. $1\frac{1}{2}$ seconds _____

6. $3\frac{2}{3}$ seconds _____

7. Another student walks at a rate of 6 feet per second. Write an equation relating seconds elapsed t and feet walked d.

_____

Name _____ **Date** _____

Remembering

Solve.

1. Sarah is beading necklaces. For every 63 seed beads she uses, she uses 7 glass beads. How many seed beads would she use if she uses 9 glass beads?

   _____

2. George is painting the outside faces of a box shaped like a rectangular prism. The dimensions of the box are 4 in. by 5 in. by 6 in. How many square inches does George paint?

   _____

Write equivalent fractions. Complete.

3.	$4\frac{2}{5}$ $3\frac{2}{3}$ $\rightarrow$	
4.	$>, <$	
5.	$+$	
6.	$-$	
7.	$\bullet$	
8.	$\div$	

Josi's dog eats 2 cups of food a day.

9. Complete the table to relate d, the number of days and c, the cups of food Josi's dog eats.

days, d	cups of food, c
1	
12	

10. Make a diagram to relate d and c.

11. Write equations to relate d and c.

   $c =$ _____ $d =$ _____

12. **Stretch Your Thinking** Keni and Bea are writing expressions for *6 more than 8 times 2*. Keni writes $(8 + 6) \bullet 2$. Bea writes $8 \bullet 2 + 6$. Is it possible to determine which expression is correct? Explain.

   _____

   _____

Formulate Equations to Relate Two Variables

Name _____ **Date** _____

Homework

SuperHero Supplies, Inc. makes a Tall-Building-Leaping Superpower soup. In the equation below, *t* is the elapsed time in seconds, and *v* is the number of liters of soup in the vat at the factory.

$$v = 4t + 2$$

1. Complete the table.

$$v = 4t + 2$$

Seconds Elapsed, *t*	Liters in Vat, *v*
0	
1	
2	
3	
4	
5	
6	

2. Plot the points from the table. Connect the points if it makes sense to.

3. Is the soup flowing at a constant rate? Explain how you found your answer.

_____

_____

4. What does the 4 in $v = 4t + 2$ tell you about this situation?

_____

_____

5. What does the 2 in $v = 4t + 2$ tell you about this situation?

_____

_____

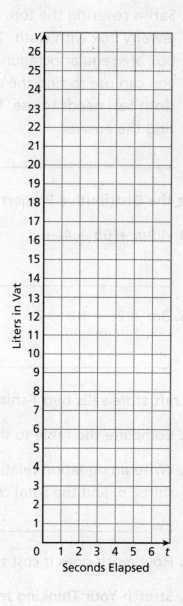

Relating Equations, Tables, and Graphs **121**

Remembering

1. For every $10 that Josephine earns, she spends $8. How much will she spend if she earns $35?

_____

2. Sari is covering the top, bottom, and sides of this jewelry box with cloth. The top and bottom of the box are regular octagons. Write an expression that you can use to find the number of square inches of cloth Sari needs to use. Then use the expression to find the answer.

_____

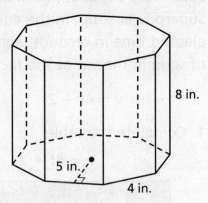

8 in.

5 in.

4 in.

Use the Distributive Property to write an equivalent expression.

3. $4(9m + 6b + 4) + r$

_____

4. $8tr + 10t + 14t^2 + 13$

_____

5. $3m + 2t - 10r - 7$

_____

6. $4y + 2x(5y + 12) + y^2$

_____

A craft store sells two T-shirts for $11.

7. Complete the table to show the cost of shirts.

8. Write an equation relating the number of shirts, n, and the total cost in dollars, t.

$t =$ _____

9. How much does it cost to buy 15 shirts? _____

number of shirts, n	total cost ($), t
1	
2	
3	
4	

10. Stretch Your Thinking Jerry buys 12 shirts for $69 at a clothing store. Write an equation to show the total cost in dollars, t, of n shirts at the clothing store. Compare your equation to the equation in Exercise 8. How do the equations show which store sells T-shirts at a less expensive price? Explain.

_____

_____

Relating Equations, Tables, and Graphs

Seward Elementary School is also considering buying bracelets from a fourth company.

Company D charges $3 for 20 bracelets, plus $2 for shipping.

1. How much does 1 bracelet cost, not including the shipping charge? Show your work.

   _____

2. How much do *n* bracelets cost, not including the shipping charge?

   _____

3. Let *n* be the number of bracelets the school buys, and let *t* be the total cost in dollars of the bracelets, including the shipping cost. Write an equation relating *t* and *n*.

   $t =$ _____

4. Explain what each term on the right side of the equation tells about this situation.

   _____

   _____

   _____

5. The cost equation for Company A is $t = 0.125n + 4$

   Does Company A or Company D offer the better price if the school buys 50 bracelets?

   _____

   Does Company A or Company D offer the better price if the school buys 200 bracelets?

   _____

Remembering

1. It takes Cheryl 16 minutes to upload 20 music files. At this rate, how many files can Cheryl upload in 40 minutes?

_____

Simplify.

2. $4.56 + 3.09$

3. $67.2 \div 21$

4. $405.4 - 65$

_____   _____   _____

The equation below shows how Mandy decides how much juice to buy for a party. In the equation, g is the number of gallons of juice she buys, and t is the length of the party in hours.

$$g = 3t + 5$$

5. Complete the table.

hours, t	gallons, g
1	
2	
3	
4	
5	

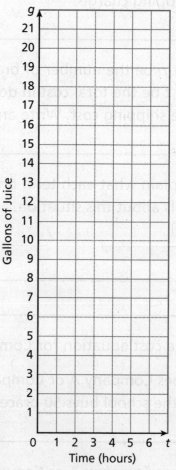

6. Plot the points from the table. Connect the points if it makes sense to do so.

7. **Stretch Your Thinking** Look at the equation above that models the amount of juice that Mandy buys for a party. What could the 3 in the equation tell you about the situation? What could the 5 tell you? Explain.

_____

_____

_____

Writing Equations

Name _____ **Date** _____

Homework

Write each statement as an inequality.

1. 10 minus 7 is less than 5. _____

2. m is greater than or equal to 25. _____

Write each inequality in words.

3. $8 > 25 \div 5$ _____

4. $9 + 5 < j$ _____

Give three solutions to each inequality.

5. $y < 11$

_____

6. $p \geq 100$

_____

7. $3 \bullet c \geq 18$

_____

8. $v + 3 > 6$

_____

Graph all the solutions of the inequality.

9. $x \leq 2$

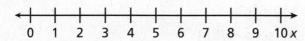

10. $w > 6$

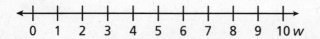

11. Customers who spend $25 or more get free shipping. Let d represent the amount spent by a customer who gets free shipping. Write an inequality to show the possible values of d.

_____

Graph the inequality to show all the possible amounts a customer who gets free shipping might spend.

```
<----+----+----+----+----+----+----+----+----+----+----+---->
     0    5   10   15   20   25   30   35   40   45   50  d
```

Remembering

1. Julian needs 20 boards to build 8 bookcases. How many bookcases can he build if he has 10 boards?

   _____

2. Gerry makes a candle shaped like the pyramid shown. The base is a regular pentagon. He paints the outside surfaces of the candle with shimmering paint. How many square centimeters does he cover with paint?

   _____

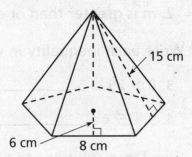
15 cm
6 cm
8 cm

Complete the equation to model the problem. Use the equation to solve the problem.

3. The fifth grade field trip costs $25 per person. What equation relates the total amount for the field trip, *t*, with the number of students going, *s*? How much is the field trip if 35 students go?

   $t =$ _____

4. Jenna is having a sidewalk sale. She pays $12 for a permit. She collects $1.50 for every item she sells. What equation relates the total amount she makes at the sale, *p*, and the number of items she sells, *i*? How much would Jenna make if she sells 25 items?

   $p =$ _____

5. **Stretch Your Thinking** Look at the situation in Exercise 4. Suppose at a second sale Jenna pays $15 for a permit and sells each item for $1.75. If she sells 30 items at each sale, at which sale does she make more money? Explain.

   _____

   _____

   _____

Inequalities

Homework

Consider these equation and inequalities:

$$\frac{2}{3}x = \frac{1}{3}x + \frac{1}{4} \qquad \frac{2}{3}x < \frac{1}{3}x + \frac{1}{4} \qquad \frac{2}{3}x > \frac{1}{3}x + \frac{1}{4}$$

1. Evaluate $\frac{2}{3}x$ for $x = \frac{1}{2}$.

_____

Evaluate $\frac{1}{3}x + \frac{1}{4}$ for $x = \frac{1}{2}$.

_____

Tell whether $x = \frac{1}{2}$ is a solution of the equation or inequality.

$\frac{2}{3}x = \frac{1}{3}x + \frac{1}{4}$ _____

$\frac{2}{3}x < \frac{1}{3}x + \frac{1}{4}$ _____

$\frac{2}{3}x > \frac{1}{3}x + \frac{1}{4}$ _____

2. Evaluate $\frac{2}{3}x$ for $x = \frac{3}{4}$.

_____

Evaluate $\frac{1}{3}x + \frac{1}{4}$ for $x = \frac{3}{4}$.

_____

Tell whether $x = \frac{3}{4}$ is a solution of the equation or inequality.

$\frac{2}{3}x = \frac{1}{3}x + \frac{1}{4}$ _____

$\frac{2}{3}x < \frac{1}{3}x + \frac{1}{4}$ _____

$\frac{2}{3}x > \frac{1}{3}x + \frac{1}{4}$ _____

3. Evaluate $\frac{2}{3}x$ for $x = 2$.

_____

Evaluate $\frac{1}{3}x + \frac{1}{4}$ for $x = 2$.

_____

Tell whether $x = 2$ is a solution of the equation or inequality.

$\frac{2}{3}x = \frac{1}{3}x + \frac{1}{4}$ _____

$\frac{2}{3}x < \frac{1}{3}x + \frac{1}{4}$ _____

$\frac{2}{3}x > \frac{1}{3}x + \frac{1}{4}$ _____

Solve the equation by thinking about what value of x will make the sides equal.

4. $3x + 94 = 21 + 94$

$x =$ _____

5. $7(x - 19) = 7 \cdot 3$

$x =$ _____

6. $145 \div 5 = (x + 8) \div 5$

$x =$ _____

Remembering

1. Anna fits 22 glass figures on 4 shelves. How many shelves does she need to fit 77 glass figures?

_____

Simplify.

2. $35 \cdot 9$

3. $2{,}431 - 1{,}944$

4. $91 \cdot 3.1$

5. $67.76 \div 1.4$

_____   _____   _____   _____

6. $344 + 12.5$

7. $378 \div 56$

8. $10.2 - 4.21$

9. $204 + 3{,}994$

_____   _____   _____   _____

Write each statement as an inequality. Then give three solutions of the inequality.

10. 7 minus 5 is less than x.

11. 8 is greater than or equal to u.

_____   _____

_____   _____

12. h is greater than 5 times 8.

13. p times 7 is less than or equal to 63.

_____   _____

_____   _____

14. Stretch Your Thinking Johnny wrote these two inequalities:

$$t < 25 \text{ and } t \geq 6 \cdot 4.$$

What could be a value of t? Explain.

_____

_____

Solutions of Equations and Inequalities

Name _____ **Date** _____

Homework

Use an inverse operation to write a related equation.
Then solve the equation for x.

1. $x - 8 = 2$ **2.** $x + 6 = 15$ **3.** $x + 4 = 5$

_____   _____   _____

4. $x - 13 = 6$ **5.** $x - 21 = 7$ **6.** $x + 14 = 34$

_____   _____   _____

Write and solve the equation each model represents.
Circle the tiles you remove from both sides.

7.

8.

_____ $x =$ _____   _____ $x =$ _____

Solve each equation using any method you choose.
Use substitution to check your answer.

9. $x - 5 = 4$ $x =$ _____   **10.** $x + 2 = 9$ $x =$ _____

11. $x - 39 = 23$ $x =$ _____   **12.** $x + 98 = 174$ $x =$ _____

13. $x + 10 = 12$ $x =$ _____   **14.** $x - 2.6 = 4$ $x =$ _____

15. $x - \frac{2}{3} = 3\frac{1}{3}$ $x =$ _____   **16.** $x + \frac{2}{3} = 5$ $x =$ _____

Remembering

1. Michelle uses 3 cups of raisins for 2 batches of cookies. How many cups of raisins does she use for 8 batches?

_____

Evaluate each expression if $u = 5$ and $v = 6$.

2. $5 \cdot (u + v) - 12$

3. $\frac{1}{2} \cdot u + 16 \div v$

_____   _____

4. $\frac{2}{3}v + \frac{1}{4}u$

5. $\frac{4}{5}(u + 3) - v$

_____   _____

6. Evaluate $\frac{1}{6}x + \frac{1}{2}$ for $x = \frac{1}{2}$.

Is $x = \frac{1}{2}$ a solution of

_____

$\frac{1}{6}x + \frac{1}{2} = 1\frac{2}{3}x$? _____

Evaluate $1\frac{2}{3}x$ for $x = \frac{1}{2}$.

$\frac{1}{6}x + \frac{1}{2} < 1\frac{2}{3}x$? _____

_____

$\frac{1}{6}x + \frac{1}{2} > 1\frac{2}{3}x$? _____

Solve the equation by thinking about what value of m will make both sides of the equation equal.

7. $4 \cdot 6 = 4(m + 4)$

8. $17 + 2m = 17 + 28$

9. $132 \div 2 = (m \cdot 12) \div 2$

$m =$ _____ $m =$ _____ $m =$ _____

10. **Stretch Your Thinking** Loretta solved the equation $5s + 10 = 10 + 60$ by thinking about what value of s makes the expressions on each side of the equation equivalent. What was Loretta's value for s? Explain.

_____

_____

Addition and Subtraction Equations

Homework

**Use an inverse operation to write a related equation.
Then solve the equation for x.**

1. $x \div 7 = 5$

_____

2. $8x = 40$

_____

3. $x \div 4 = 6$

_____

4. $9x = 63$

_____

5. $x \div 2 = 13$

_____

6. $10x = 50$

_____

Write and solve the equation each model represents.

7.

_____

8.

_____

**Solve each equation using any method. Use
substitution to check your answer.**

9. $12x = 84$ $x = $ _____

10. $x \div 8 = 16$ $x = $ _____

11. $\frac{1}{5}x = 30$ $x = $ _____

12. $2.5x = 20$ $x = $ _____

13. $\frac{x}{6} = 6$ $x = $ _____

14. $\frac{5}{6}x = 5$ $x = $ _____

15. $3x = 22.5$ $x = $ _____

16. $\frac{x}{4} = 17$ $x = $ _____

Name _____ **Date** _____

Remembering

Solve.

1. Bonnie buys yarn to use to crochet. At the first store, she can buy 8 packages for $10. At a second store she can buy 32 of the same size packages for $44. Which store has the less expensive price?

_____

Write equivalent fractions. Complete.

2.	$\frac{5}{12}$ $\frac{3}{8}$ $\rightarrow$	
3.	$>, <$	
4.	$+$	
5.	$-$	
6.	$\bullet$	
7.	$\div$	

Simplify each expression.

8. $12e + 37 + 5(e - 6) + 2$

_____

9. $\frac{1}{2}(12 + n) + 4n - 3$

_____

10. $g(12 + g) - 9g - 17$

_____

11. $2y(3y) + 16(y + 2) - 10$

_____

Solve each equation.

12. $16 = 4 + p$ $p =$ _____

13. $r - 3.4 = 10.7$ $r =$ _____

14. $x + 2\frac{2}{5} = 10\frac{1}{2}$ $x =$ _____

15. $y - 10.2 = 6$ $y =$ _____

16. $u - 5\frac{1}{6} = 8$ $u =$ _____

17. $18 = k + 12$ $k =$ _____

18. **Stretch Your Thinking** Use addition to write an equation that you can use to find the perimeter, P, of a rectangle with length 6 m and width 14.6 m. Then use the equation to find the perimeter.

_____

Multiplication and Division Equations

Homework

The table below illustrates the cost of a taxi ride for various distances. The total cost includes a fixed $5 initial charge, and a cost for every one-tenth of a mile traveled.

Cost of a Taxi Ride			
Distance in Miles (d)	Mileage Cost in Dollars	Initial Charge in Dollars	Total Cost in Dollars (t)
$\frac{1}{10}$	1	5	6
$\frac{1}{5}$			
$\frac{1}{2}$			
$\frac{7}{10}$			
1			

Solve.

1. One cost is the initial charge in dollars. What is the other cost?

   _____

   _____

2. Complete the table.

3. Graph the data for distance and total cost.

4. Write an equation that can be used to find the total cost in dollars (t) of a ride for any distance in miles (d).

   _____

5. Predict the cost of a $2\frac{1}{2}$ mile ride. Use the equation you wrote in Exercise 4 to check your prediction.

   _____

Focus on Mathematical Practices

Remembering

1. During a week, for every 2 miles that Leigh runs, she walks 3 miles. How many miles will Leigh walk if she runs 10 miles?

_____

Simplify.

2. $6.56 \div 16$

3. $72 \cdot 14$

4. $809 + 1.2$

_____ _____ _____

5. $7,125 - 2,034$

6. $0.344 \cdot 0.2$

7. $0.729 \div 0.45$

_____ _____ _____

Use the Distributive Property to write an equivalent expression.

8. $3(15 + 11)$

9. $34a + 12ab$

_____ _____

10. $8x(4 + 2b) + 10$

11. $3q + 12w + 4w^2$

_____ _____

Solve each equation.

12. $\frac{1}{2}h = 24$ $h = $ _____

13. $16 = 2w$ $w = $ _____

14. $x \div 12 = 9.2$ $x = $ _____

15. $8 = \frac{3}{4}b$ $b = $ _____

16. Stretch Your Thinking Use multiplication to write an equation that you can use to find the width, w, of a rectangle with length 9 ft and area 127.8 ft^2. Then use the equation to find the width.

_____

Name _____ **Date** _____

Homework

Find the surface area and volume.

1.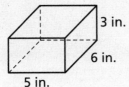
3 in.
6 in.
5 in.

2.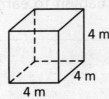
4 m
4 m
4 m

3.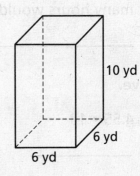
10 yd
6 yd
6 yd

SA = _____   SA = _____   SA = _____

V = _____   V = _____   V = _____

Choose the most appropriate measure. Write _perimeter,_
surface area, **or** _volume._

4. the distance around the shopping mall _____

5. the amount of topsoil needed to put a 2 in. thick layer on the
   top of a square garden _____

6. the amount of siding needed for a house _____

Solve.

7. How many inch cubes would it take to fill the
   aquarium? What is the open surface area
   of the water?

   _____

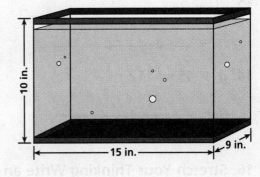
10 in.
15 in.
9 in.

8. For good health, a 2 in. long fish requires
   48 in.² of open surface area. How many fish
   about 2 in. long could be kept in an aquarium
   with an open surface that is 16 in. by 21 in.?

   _____

9. The volume of an aquarium for one fish is 384 cubic inches.
   The height of the aquarium is 6 inches. The base is a square.
   What are the dimensions of the base?

   _____

Remembering

1. Julie babysits for 10 hours and earns $45. At that rate, how many hours would she need to babysit to earn $72?

_____

Solve.

2. 4.55 • 13

_____

3. 23.4 ÷ 6

_____

4. 3,094 + 1,229

_____

5. 7,299 − 6,459

_____

6. 0.095 • 0.03

_____

7. 0.03402 ÷ 0.09

_____

Solve each equation.

8. $\frac{3}{4} + y = 1\frac{2}{3}$

   $y =$ _____

9. $8 = \frac{2}{5}u$

   $u =$ _____

10. $p - 9.3 = 29.4$

   $p =$ _____

11. $t \div 1\frac{3}{4} = 4\frac{1}{2}$

   $t =$ _____

12. $\frac{h}{14} = 24$

   $h =$ _____

13. $8\frac{1}{2} = \frac{3}{4} + b$

   $b =$ _____

14. $g + 45 = 112$

   $g =$ _____

15. $5.4m = 24.3$

   $m =$ _____

16. Stretch Your Thinking Write an equation that can be used to find the height, h, of a rectangular prism with length 5 cm, width 3 cm, and surface area 62 cm². Then use the equation to find the height of the prism. Show your work.

_____

_____

_____

What Is Volume?

Find the volume.

1.

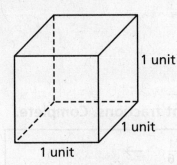

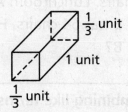

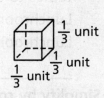

| Unit Cube | Prism D | Prism E | Prism F |

$V =$ _____ $V =$ _____ $V =$ _____ $V =$ _____

2.

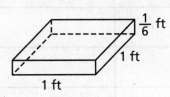

3.

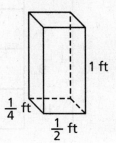

4.

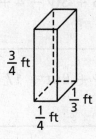

$V =$ _____ $V =$ _____ $V =$ _____

5.

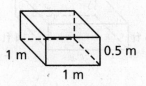

6.

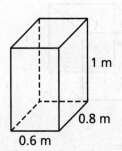

7.

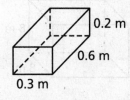

$V =$ _____ $V =$ _____ $V =$ _____

Solve.

8. A plastic box in the shape of a rectangular prism has a base that is $\frac{7}{2}$ in. by $\frac{5}{2}$ in. and a height of $\frac{1}{2}$ in. How many cubes with edge lengths of $\frac{1}{2}$ in. would it take to fill the plastic box? What is the volume of the prism? _____

9. Describe two different rectangular prisms each of which has the volume $\frac{8}{100}$ ft³.

_____

_____

Name _____ **Date** _____

Remembering

1. Lunchroom A and Lunchroom B have the same ratio of tables to chairs. Lunchroom A has 7 tables and 42 chairs. Lunchroom B has 54 chairs. How many tables are in Lunchroom B?

_____

Simplify by combining like terms. Use the Distributive Property if possible.

2. $4r + t(r + 6) + 7t$

_____

3. $15 + 3(y - 4 + g) - 2g$

_____

4. $6y + 8ut + 17 - 4y - 10$

_____

Write equivalent fractions. Complete.

5.	$3\frac{3}{8}$	$3\frac{1}{6}$ $\rightarrow$	
6.	>, <		
7.	+		
8.	–		
9.	•		
10.	÷		

Find the surface area and volume.

11.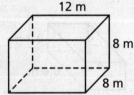

12 m, 8 m, 8 m

SA = _____

V = _____

12.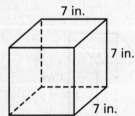

7 in., 7 in., 7 in.

SA = _____

V = _____

13.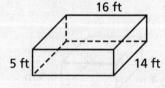

16 ft, 5 ft, 14 ft

SA = _____

V = _____

14. **Stretch Your Thinking** When Carrie calculated the surface area and the volume of a rectangular prism, she got the same number. Only the measurement units were different. Describe Carrie's figure. Explain your answer.

_____

_____

_____

_____

Fractional Unit Cubes

Homework

1. Draw a base for a prism on the centimeter grid below. Choose a fractional height. Visualize the prism. Then write an expression for the volume of the prism using those dimensions.

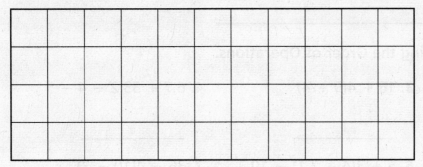

_____

2. Explain the volume of the prism in Exercise 1 in terms of layers of cubes.

_____

_____

3. Calculate the volume of the prism you visualized in Exercise 1.

_____

Find the volume.

4.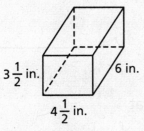

$V =$ _____

5.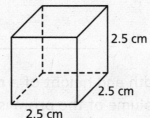

$V =$ _____

6.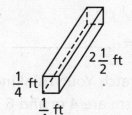

$V =$ _____

Find the unknown dimension.

7. A rectangular prism has a volume of 7.875 m³ and a height of 3.5 m. What is the area of the base of the prism?

_____

8. A rectangular prism has a volume of 9 in.³ The area of the base is 4 in.² What is the height of the prism?

Remembering

1. Jeremiah got 8 out of 10 problems correct on his test. Mariah got 36 out of 40 problems correct on her test. Who got the greater fraction of their problems correct?

_____

Simplify each expression using the Order of Operations.

2. $7 + 3^2 \cdot 2$

3. $16 + 4(9 + 4)$

4. $6.7 + 33.2 \div 4 - 5$

_____   _____   _____

5. $(4 + 5)^2 - 2 \cdot 12$

6. $5 + 3(4 + 2.1) - 10.3$

7. $36 - 4(10 - 3)$

_____   _____   _____

Find the volume.

8.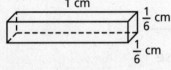

9.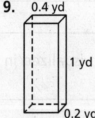

10.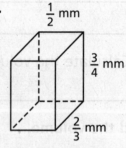

$V =$ _____ $V =$ _____ $V =$ _____

11. **Stretch Your Thinking** The width and height of a rectangular prism are 4 m and 6 m. The volume of the prism is 12 m³. What is the length of the prism? Explain.

_____

_____

_____

_____

_____

Compose Rectangular Prisms with Fractional Edge Lengths

Homework

**Write a numerical expression for the volume.
Then calculate the volume.**

1.
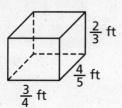

$\frac{2}{3}$ ft

$\frac{4}{5}$ ft

$\frac{3}{4}$ ft

2.
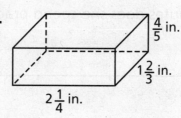

$\frac{4}{5}$ in.

$1\frac{2}{3}$ in.

$2\frac{1}{4}$ in.

3.
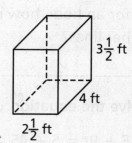

$3\frac{1}{2}$ ft

4 ft

$2\frac{1}{2}$ ft

V = _____

V = _____

V = _____

Find the unknown dimension or volume of each rectangular prism.

4. $l = 4\frac{1}{2}$ in.

 $w = 1\frac{1}{3}$ in.

 $h = \frac{3}{4}$ in.

 $V = $ _____

5. $V = 25\frac{3}{5}$ yd³

 $w = 3\frac{1}{5}$ yd

 $h = 2\frac{1}{2}$ yd

 $l = $ _____

6. $l = 6$ ft

 $w = 3\frac{1}{2}$ ft

 $V = 49$ ft³

 $h = $ _____

7. $l = 4.6$ cm

 $h = 3.4$ cm

 $w = 2.5$ cm

 $V = $ _____

Solve.

8. A rectangular storage container has a base that measures 1.2 m by 3 m and is 2.4 m high. What is the volume of the storage container?

_____

9. A sand box is 3 ft by 4 ft and 6 in. tall. How many cubic feet of sand does the sand box hold?

_____

10. A lunch box has a volume of 221 in.³ The height is 4 in. and the width is $6\frac{1}{2}$ in. What is the length?

_____

Name _____ **Date** _____

Remembering

1. At play practice, Sarah spends 12 minutes out of every 20 minutes practicing her lines. If Sarah is at play practice for an hour, how many minutes does she spend practicing her lines?

_____

Solve the equation.

2. $5 + 9t = 5 + 45$

    $t =$ _____

3. $8 + 2 = 2 + 4y$

    $y =$ _____

4. $\frac{r}{16} = 32$

    $r =$ _____

5. $\frac{5}{7} + j = 1\frac{2}{5}$

    $j =$ _____

Find the volume.

6.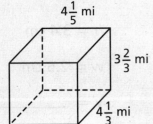

    $4\frac{1}{5}$ mi, $3\frac{2}{3}$ mi, $4\frac{1}{3}$ mi

7.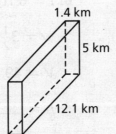

    1.4 km, 5 km, 12.1 km

8.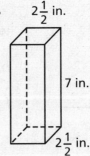

    $2\frac{1}{2}$ in., 7 in., $2\frac{1}{2}$ in.

$V =$ _____ $V =$ _____ $V =$ _____

9. **Stretch Your Thinking** Write an equation that you can use to represent the volume of a square prism. Use b to represent the length and width of the base. Use h to represent the height of the prism. Use exponents if possible. Then explain your answer.

_____

_____

_____

_____

Volume of Prisms with Fractional Edge Lengths

Homework

Write an equation for volume, V, using the variables given.

1. Each edge of a cube is f feet long. If V is the volume of the cube, write an equation relating f and V.

_____

2. A rectangular prism has a square base with edge lengths e and height r. Write an equation relating e, r, and V.

_____

3. A rectangular prism is 6 cm tall and has a base of area C cm². Write an equation relating C and V.

_____

Solve.   *Show your work.*

4. A shipping box is $\frac{2}{3}$ filled with peanuts. The shipping box has length $10\frac{1}{2}$ in., width $8\frac{1}{2}$ in., and height 12 in. What is the volume of the peanuts?

_____

5. The length of an aquarium is 13 in. The width is $\frac{1}{2}$ of the length. The height is $1\frac{1}{2}$ in. more that the width. What is the volume of the aquarium?

_____

6. The sum of the areas of the top and bottom of a cereal box is 32 cm². The box is 4 times as long as it is wide. What is the length of the box?

_____

7. Topsoil costs $8 a cubic yard. How much will it cost to put 12 in. of topsoil on a 6 yd by 7 yd garden?

_____

8. A box of pencils has length $8\frac{1}{2}$ in., width $3\frac{1}{2}$ in., and height $\frac{1}{2}$ in. What is the greatest number of boxes of pencils that will fit in a shipping box that has a base $1\frac{1}{2}$ ft by $1\frac{1}{6}$ ft and a height of 1 ft?

_____

Remembering

1. It takes Johab 32 minutes to print 20 pictures. At this rate, how many pictures can Johab print in 1 hour and 12 minutes?

_____

Solve.

2. 1,893 ÷ 345

_____

3. 1.02 • 16

_____

4. 69.23 + 1.22

_____

5. 4.67 • 1.1

_____

6. 34.529 ÷ 0.043

_____

7. 10,343 − 9,844

_____

Write a numerical expression for the volume.
Then calculate the volume.

8.

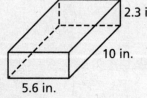

2.3 in.
10 in.
5.6 in.

9.

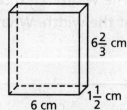

$6\frac{2}{3}$ cm
$1\frac{1}{2}$ cm
6 cm

10.

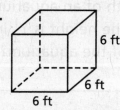

6 ft
6 ft
6 ft

V = _____   V = _____   V = _____

11. Stretch Your Thinking The volume of a square prism is 67.5 m³. The height of the prism is 7.5 m. What are the dimensions of the base of the prism? Explain.

_____

_____

_____

_____

Write and Solve Equations about Volume

Homework

A design for a rectangular goldfish pond, with an area for landscaping, a safety fence, and a sidewalk next to the fence on the outside is needed for a shopping mall.

1. Draw a design below for the goldfish pond and the area around it. Label the dimensions on your design. Remember to include the depth of the pond.

2. Use your drawing to find the perimeter of the fence, the area of the sidewalk, and the volume of the goldfish pond.

_____

_____

_____

Remembering

The equation below shows the amount of money Park spends at the store. In the equation, c is the number of baseball cards he buys and t is the total amount he spends.

$$t = 1.5c + 6$$

1. Complete the table.

$$t = 1.5c + 6$$

cards, c	total ($), t
1	
2	
3	
4	
5	

2. Plot the points from the table. Connect the points if it makes sense to.

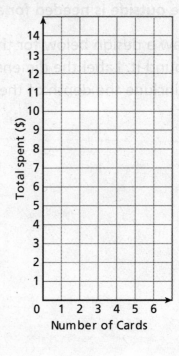

Solve.

3. Jacqueline earns $88 mowing 16 lawns. At this rate, how much does she get paid to mow 6 lawns?

_____

4. The sum of the areas of the top and bottom of a cabinet is 54 ft². The height of the cabinet is 5 ft. What is the volume of the cabinet?

_____

5. **Stretch Your Thinking** Janaya is planning to build a toy box. She makes a sketch of the toy box and finds the volume. Then she doubles each dimension of the box and finds the volume of the larger box. Write equations to show the relationship between the volume of the small box and the volume of the large box. Explain your answer.

_____

_____

_____

Homework

1. Complete these ratio tables for two paint mixtures.

Peacock Purple	
Red	Blue
2	5
	15
14	

Purple Plum	
Red	Blue
7	3
	15
14	

2. Which paint is more red? _____

3. Which paint is less red? _____

4. Graph two points from each table. Draw and label a line for *Peacock Purple* and a line for *Purple Plum*.

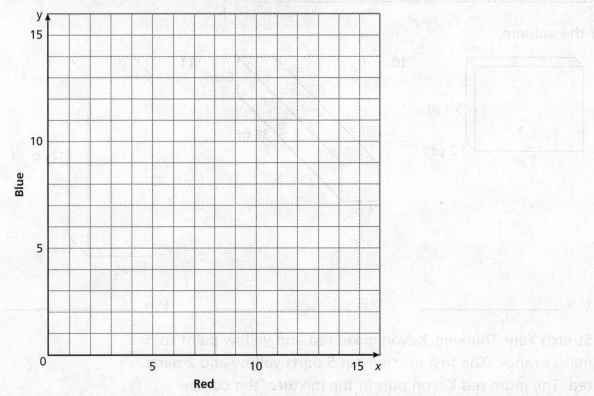

5. Explain how to use the two lines on the graph and a straightedge to determine which paint is more blue.

_____

_____

_____

Remembering

Solve.

1. It takes Elizabeth 15 minutes to walk 5 blocks. At that rate, how many minutes will it take her to walk 30 blocks?

_____

2. Anyola is making a box out of cardboard. The box is in the shape of a hexagonal pyramid. The side length of the regular hexagonal base is 14 in. and the distance to the center is 12 in. The height of a triangular face is 20 in. How much cardboard does she need to make the box?

_____

Write equivalent fractions. Complete.

3.	$\frac{3}{8}$ $\frac{1}{10}$ →	
4.	>, <	
5.	+	
6.	−	
7.	•	
8.	÷	

Find the volume.

9.
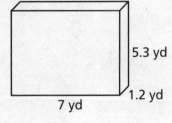
5.3 yd
1.2 yd
7 yd

10.
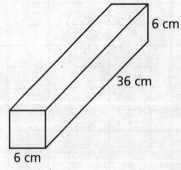
6 cm
36 cm
6 cm

11.
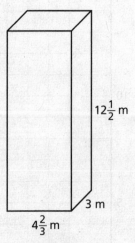
6 cm
$12\frac{1}{2}$ m
3 m
$4\frac{2}{3}$ m

V = _____

V = _____

V = _____

12. **Stretch Your Thinking** Kevon mixes red and yellow paint to make orange. The first mixture has 5 parts yellow and 2 parts red. The more red Kevon puts in the mixture, the darker the color. Kevon wants to make an orange paint that is darker than his first mixture. How many parts of red should he mix with 10 parts yellow? Explain your answer.

_____

_____

Solve.

1. Grammy Suzy's recipe for summer salad is 2 cucumbers for every 3 tomatoes. How many tomatoes are in a salad with 5 cucumbers?

   _____

2. Eighteen of Susan's muffins weigh the same as 15 of Tom's muffins. How many of Susan's muffins weigh the same as 7 of Tom's muffins?

   _____

3. Foster Publishers' printing press can print 5 dictionaries in 8 minutes. How many dictionaries can it print in 10 minutes?

   _____

4. A turtle crawled 21 meters in 12 minutes. How long did it take her to crawl 14 meters if she crawled at the same rate the whole time?

   _____

Remembering

1. Roger averages 3 hits for every 12 times he is at bat. At this rate, how many times must he bat to get 12 hits?

_____

2. A box is $\frac{3}{4}$ filled with raisins. The box has length $5\frac{1}{2}$ inches, width $3\frac{1}{2}$ in., and height 7 in. What is the volume of the raisins?

_____

Complete the ratio tables for the two recipes.

3. Grandma's Sweet and Salty Trail Mix

Salt	Brown Sugar
3	2
15	
	8

4. Aunt Em's Sweet and Salty Trail Mix

Salt	Brown Sugar
4	5
	10
12	

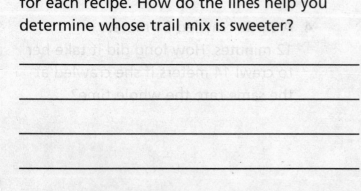

5. Whose recipe is saltier? _____

6. Whose recipe is sweeter? _____

7. Graph two points from each table. Draw a line for each recipe. How do the lines help you determine whose trail mix is sweeter?

_____

_____

_____

_____

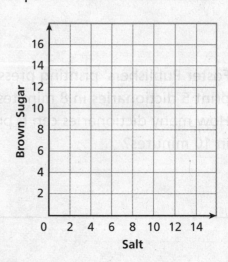

8. Stretch Your Thinking Edney wants to make a recipe for trail mix that is saltier than Aunt Em's but not as salty as Grandma's. What ratio of salt to brown sugar could Edney use? Use the graph above to help you. Explain.

_____

_____

_____

Unit Rates

Homework

Name _____ Date _____

1. Complete the ratio table.

Cups of Juice

Berry			1	4	6
Orange		1		10		40

a. The basic ratio of $\frac{\text{berry}}{\text{orange}}$ is _____.

b. There is _____ cup of berry juice for every cup of orange juice.

c. The basic ratio of $\frac{\text{orange}}{\text{berry}}$ is _____.

d. There are _____ cups of orange juice for every cup of berry juice.

Solve each proportion.

2. $\frac{24}{15} = \frac{a}{35}$

3. $\frac{b}{15} = \frac{8}{20}$

4. $\frac{4}{9} = \frac{r}{6}$

$a =$ _____ $b =$ _____ $r =$ _____

Solve each problem using ratios in fraction notation.

5. Fifteen 2-inch nails weigh 35 grams. How many of these nails weigh 175 grams?

6. Five yards of shirt fabric cost $9. How much do 12 yards of the same fabric cost?

_____   _____

Name _____ **Date** _____

Remembering

1. Merril is making a box out of cardstock. A diagram of the box is shown. Merril will fill the box with number cubes each $1\frac{1}{2}$ in. on an edge. How much cardstock does Merril need for the box? How many number cubes can Merril fit in the box?

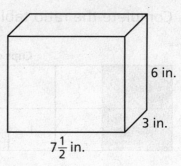

6 in.

3 in.

$7\frac{1}{2}$ in.

_____

Solve the equation or evaluate the expression for $b = 4$ and $c = 5$.

2. $\frac{2}{3}g = 45$

3. $7(c^2 - b \cdot 3) + 10$

4. $b + c \cdot b + b - (b + c)$

$g =$ _____

_____

_____

5. $6 + 2t = 10$

6. $\frac{y}{32} = 12$

7. $(7 + b)^2 - c \cdot b$

$t =$ _____

$y =$ _____

_____

Solve.

8. At a bakery, a baker prepares 6 dozen blueberry muffins for every 5 dozen apple muffins. If the baker prepares 16 dozen blueberry muffins, how many dozen apple muffins will he prepare?

_____

9. A rabbit hopped 11 meters in 6 minutes. At that rate, how far did the rabbit hop in 8 minutes?

_____

10. **Stretch Your Thinking** Jeremy and April are braiding a rug. Jeremy makes 4 braids every 11 minutes. April makes 7 braids every 17 minutes. Who is braiding at a faster rate? Explain.

_____

_____

Ratios, Fractions, and Fraction Notation

Name _____ **Date** _____

Homework

Solve each proportion. Use any method.

1. $\frac{7}{4} = \frac{12}{a}$

2. $\frac{10}{15} = \frac{c}{18}$

3. $\frac{9}{r} = \frac{6}{8}$

$a =$ _____ $c =$ _____ $r =$ _____

Solve each problem. Use any method.

4. Lemon Yellow paint can be made by mixing 5 gallons of yellow paint and 2 gallons of white paint. How many gallons of yellow paint should be mixed with 9 gallons of white paint to make Lemon Yellow?

5. Bill's trail mix has 6 cups of walnuts and 10 cups of cranberries. Using the same recipe, how many cups of walnuts go with 15 cups of cranberries?

_____

6. Mrs. Lee uses 9 cups of water for every 2 cups of rice. How many cups of water are needed for 5 cups of rice?

7. Doris bought 15 yards of fabric for $7. How much do 6 yards of the same fabric cost?

_____

_____

Understanding Cross-Multiplication **153**

Name _____ **Date** _____

Remembering

1. Mr. O'Neil is installing wood flooring to cover the area shown. Write an expression that you can use to find the amount of flooring he needs. Then use the expression to find the amount of flooring.

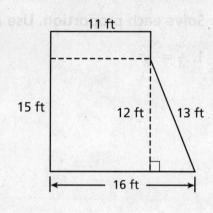

_____

_____

Find the value of n.

2. $4.5 \cdot 11 = n$

3. $n = 6.774 \div 12$

4. $n = 56 \cdot 1.2$

$n =$ _____

$n =$ _____

$n =$ _____

5. $\frac{n}{25} = \frac{3}{15}$

6. $\frac{20}{n} = \frac{45}{54}$

7. $\frac{36}{32} = \frac{n}{64}$

$n =$ _____

$n =$ _____

$n =$ _____

Solve.

8. There are 40 feet of ribbon in 12 packages. How many feet of ribbon are in 21 packages?

_____

9. Six boxes of crackers cost $20. At this price, how much do 15 boxes cost?

_____

10. **Stretch Your Thinking** The table shows how much two friends spent for deli meat at different stores. Jaime spent less per pound than Philip, but more per pound than Shazad. If Jaime bought 5 lb of deli meat, how much could she have spent? Explain.

Cost of Deli Meat	
Philip	2 lb for $5
Shazad	4 lb for $9

_____

_____

_____

_____

_____

_____

Understanding Cross-Multiplication

Homework

To make Glowing Green paint, blue and yellow paint are mixed in a ratio of 3 to 4.

Draw tape diagrams to help you solve these problems.

Show your work.

1. How much yellow paint should a store mix with 15 liters of blue paint to make Glowing Green paint?

2. How much blue paint and yellow paint should a store mix to make 98 gallons of Glowing Green paint?

3. How much blue paint should a store mix with 17 quarts of yellow paint to make Glowing Green paint?

4. How much blue and yellow paint should a store mix to make 50 gallons of Glowing Green paint?

Remembering

1. Centra bought a dress and three shirts. The dress cost $24.50. The shirts cost $11.50 each. How much did Centra spend?

_____

Use the Distributive Property to simplify each expression.

2. $6(m + 7 + t) + 6m - 2t$ 3. $x(x + 23) - 10x + 3x^2$ 4. $10 + 5(a + b) - 5a$

_____   _____   _____

5. $7st + 4t(s + t + 4) - 9t$ 6. $4 \cdot 3s + 7 \cdot 2s$ 7. $15 + 7r + r(r - 3) - r^2$

_____   _____   _____

Solve.

8. Gerri's recipe calls for 8 carrots for every 5 servings. How many carrots are needed for 15 servings?

_____

9. The cast of the play makes 275 programs for 5 shows. How many programs will be needed for 13 shows?

_____

10. Marisa needs 8 gallons of lemonade for every 60 guests that come to her party. If she is inviting 25 guests, how many gallons of lemonade does she need?

_____

11. Ned can buy 12 juice boxes for $4.80. At that price, how many juice boxes can he buy for $24?

_____

12. **Stretch Your Thinking** Juju is making punch for a picnic. She uses 0.75 liter of apple juice and 1.2 liters of grape juice. By mistake, she adds an extra 0.3 liter of apple juice to the punch bowl before putting in any grape juice. How many liters of grape juice should she add to the bowl so that the ingredients will be in the original ratio? Explain.

_____

_____

_____

Describing Ratios with Tape Diagrams

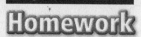

Edmundo made a salad dressing by mixing mayonnaise and ketchup in a ratio of 2 to 3.

1. Draw a tape diagram for the mixture.

For Exercises 2–6, complete the sentences to describe Edmundo's mixture.

2. There are _____ parts ketchup in _____ parts of the mixture.

3. Mayonnaise and ketchup are mixed in a ratio of _____ to _____ or _____ : _____.

4. The amount of ketchup is _____ times as much as the amount of mayonnaise.

5. The amount of mayonnaise is _____ times as much as the amount of ketchup.

6. The amount of the mixture is _____ times as much as the amount of ketchup.

7. Let K be the number of milliliters of ketchup.
Let M be the number of milliliters of mayonnaise.
Write two equations relating K and M.

_____

Lee made a salad dressing by mixing oil and vinegar in a ratio of 7 to 2.

8. Draw a tape diagram for the mixture.

For Exercises 9–13, complete the sentences to describe Lee's mixture.

9. There are _____ parts oil in _____ parts of the mixture.

10. Oil and vinegar are mixed in a ratio of _____ to _____ or _____ : _____.

11. The amount of oil is _____ times as much as the amount of vinegar.

12. The amount of vinegar is _____ times as much as the amount of oil.

13. The amount of the mixture is _____ times as much as the amount of oil.

14. Let L be the number of milliliters of oil.
Let V be the number of milliliters of vinegar.
Write two equations relating L and V.

Remembering

Write each word expression as an algebraic expression.

1. the sum of 5 and u

_____

2. Divide 7 more than t by 3.

_____

3. Subtract $\frac{2}{5}$ from the product of 4 and s.

_____

4. Divide $\frac{2}{3}$ by y.

_____

To make banana berry smoothies, Just Juice mixes water and juice in a ratio of 5 to 3. Draw tape diagrams to help you solve these problems.

5. How much water and juice should Just Juice mix to make 104 quarts of banana berry smoothies?

_____

_____

6. How much water should Just Juice mix with 23 gallons of juice to make banana berry smoothies?

_____

7. Stretch Your Thinking To make Citrus Orange paint, a paint store mixes yellow, white, and red paint in the ratio of 5 to 3 to 1. How many gallons of yellow, white, and red paint does the store need to mix to make 135 gallons of Citrus Orange paint?

_____

_____

Ratios and Multiplicative Comparisons

Homework

Solve. Use different methods including tables, Factor Puzzles, cross-multiplication, and tape diagrams. Look for the problem that cannot be solved with any of these!

Show your work.

1. A box of laundry detergent costs $12 and can be used for 50 loads of laundry. How much does the detergent for 7 loads of laundry cost?

   _____

2. Mr. Parker will mix antifreeze and water in a ratio of 2 to 1. He needs 27 quarts of the antifreeze and water mixture to fill his car's radiator. How much antifreeze and how much water should Mr. Parker mix together?

   Antifreeze: _____ Water: _____

3. Marta and Nicole run laps around the track. They run at the same constant speed but Marta starts first. When Marta has run 5 laps, Nicole has run 3 laps. How many laps will Nicole have run when Marta has run 8 laps?

   _____

4. Pokey the snail travels 25 centimeters every 2 minutes. How long will it take Pokey to go 60 centimeters?

   _____

5. If a 3-pound bag of oranges costs $5, how many pounds of oranges should you be able to buy for $12?

   _____

6. At a perfume factory, fragrance designers are making Green Blossom perfume by mixing new grass fragrance with $\frac{3}{4}$ times as much apple blossom fragrance. How much new grass fragrance and apple blossom fragrance will they need to mix to make 1 liter of Green Blossom perfume?

   New grass: _____ Apple blossom: _____

Remembering

1. Marilou is making a collage using a trapezoid pattern. The area of her shape is 27.3 in.². The length of one base is 7 in. and the height is 6 in. What is the length of the other base?

_____

2. A flower vase is shaped like a rectangular prism. The base of the vase is 11 in. by 8 in. The vase is $\frac{2}{3}$ full. There are 704 in.³ of water in the vase. What is the height of the vase?

_____

Nathan mixes 5 parts water with 2 parts liquid plant food.

3. Draw a tape diagram for the mixture.

4. What is the ratio of water to food? food to water?

water to food: _____

food to water: _____

5. How many times the amount of water is the amount of food?

_____

6. How many times the amount of food is the amount of water?

_____

7. Let w be the number of cups of water. Let f be the number of cups of plant food. Write two equations relating w and f.

_____   _____

8. **Stretch Your Thinking** Millie and Leo drew rectangular prisms. The ratio of the volume of Millie's prism to the volume of Leo's prism is 5:4. If the dimensions of Millie's prism are 3 in., 6 in., and 10 in., what could be the dimensions of Leo's prism? Explain.

_____

_____

_____

_____

Homework

1. Write each percent as a fraction with denominator 100 and as a decimal. Then place the percents and decimals on the number lines.

Percent	42%	71%	80%	8%	88%	108%
Fraction						
Decimal						

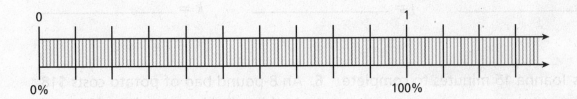

What percent of the figure is shaded?

2. _____

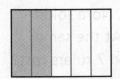

3. _____

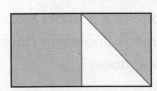

4. _____

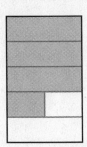

5. _____

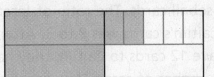

6. _____

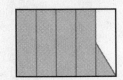

7. _____

Remembering

1. Bonnie runs $1\frac{2}{3}$ times as far as John each day. If Bonnie runs 5 miles on Monday, $3\frac{1}{2}$ miles on Tuesday, and $5\frac{3}{4}$ miles on Wednesday, how many miles did John run in all those three days?

_____

Solve each equation.

2. $7y = 34$

3. $\frac{j}{15} = 20$

4. $\frac{5}{6}k = \frac{4}{7}$

$y = $ _____ $j = $ _____ $k = $ _____

Solve.

5. It takes Joanna 15 minutes to complete 4 puzzles. At that rate, how many puzzles can she complete in 1 hour 45 minutes?

_____

6. An 8-pound bag of potato costs $18. At this price, how much would 15 pounds of potatoes cost?

_____

7. Sarah can fit 115 books in 2 bookcases. At that rate, how many bookcases does she need to hold 360 books?

_____

8. At a math convention, Nora sold 13 rulers for $110.50. At the same price, how much would 7 rulers cost?

_____

9. **Stretch Your Thinking** Jeremy and Caitlin collect baseball cards. The ratio of Jeremy's cards to Caitlin's cards was 9 to 3. After Jeremy gave 12 cards to Caitlin, they had an equal number of cards. How many cards did Caitlin and Jeremy have at first? Explain.

_____

_____

_____

_____

The Meaning of Percent

Name **Date**

Homework

The 400 dogs at a shelter are in 100 groups of 4.

1. Color 7% of the dogs. How many dogs is this?

_____

2. Color 65% of dogs with a different color. How many dogs is this?

_____

3. What is 98% of 700 cats? Solve this in two ways.

4. What is 22% of 500 birds? Solve this in two ways.

_____

Percent of a Number **163**

Remembering

1. Gabby sold 24 bracelets for $126. How much would 35 bracelets cost?

_____

Solve each proportion.

2. $\frac{8}{10} = \frac{16}{y}$

3. $\frac{6}{7} = \frac{4}{y}$

4. $\frac{12}{y} = \frac{19}{4}$

$y =$ _____ $y =$ _____ $y =$ _____

Tell what percent of the figure is shaded. Then write the percent as a fraction with denominator 100 and as a decimal.

5.

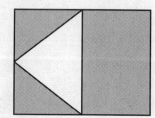

Percent: _____

Fraction: _____

Decimal: _____

6.

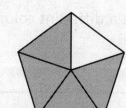

Percent: _____

Fraction: _____

Decimal: _____

7.

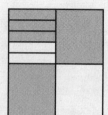

Percent: _____

Fraction: _____

Decimal: _____

8.

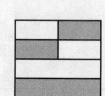

Percent: _____

Fraction: _____

Decimal: _____

9. **Stretch Your Thinking** Vanessa shaded 55% of her picture red. Did she shade more or less than $\frac{2}{5}$ of the picture? Explain.

_____

_____

Homework

Solve in two ways.   *Show your work.*

1. Mr. Wallace took 600 mg of medicine. This was 75% of the full dose. What is the full dose?

_____

2. A full dose of a different medicine is 600 mg. Ms. Mehta took 75% of a full dose. How much medicine did she take?

_____

3. Daniel has read 180 pages. This is 80% of the entire book. How long is the book?

_____

4. Lauren's book is 180 pages long. She has read 80% of it. How many pages has she read?

_____

5. What is 20% of 90?   **6.** 20% of what number is 90?

_____   _____

7. 60% of what number is 150?   **8.** What is 60% of 150?

_____   _____

Remembering

1. On a certain TV station, there are 4 commercials during every 30-minute period. How many minutes of TV do you need to watch to have watched more than 10 commercials?

   _____

2. The width of a box of trail mix is $\frac{1}{2}$ its height. The height is $2\frac{1}{2}$ in. more than its length. If the length of the box is 8 in., how much trail mix does the box hold?

   _____

Write each statement as an inequality. Then give three solutions of the inequality.

3. 3 times 7 is less than or equal to x.

   _____

   _____

4. 16 is greater than $u + 2$.

   _____

   _____

5. h is greater than 4 fewer than 6.

   _____

   _____

6. p divided by 3 is greater than or equal to 12.

   _____

   _____

Solve.

7. What is 55% of 300 trees?

   _____

8. What is 30% of 800 children?

   _____

9. What is 63% of 500 actors?

   _____

10. What is 88% of 600 shirts?

    _____

11. **Stretch Your Thinking** Alice's book has 200 pages. Alice has read 75% of the pages in her book. Nina has read the same number of pages but only 50% of the pages in her book. How many pages are in Nina's book? Explain.

    _____

    _____

Homework

Solve.

Show your work.

1. If 560 mg is 80% of a dose of medicine, how much is a full dose?

   _____

2. If a full dose of medicine is 560 mg, how much is 80% of a dose?

   _____

3. A patient was supposed to take 560 mg of medicine but took only 420 mg. What percent of the medicine did the patient take?

   _____

4. If the sales tax is 7%, how much tax will you pay on a CD that costs $15?

   _____

5. In Smallville, 2,400 out of 20,000 workers are unemployed. In Bigtown, 6,750 out of 75,000 workers are unemployed. Which town has a larger unemployment problem? Why?

   _____

   _____

6. Four out of every 5 dentists recommend Sparkle toothpaste. What percent of dentists recommend Sparkle toothpaste?

   _____

7. The recommended daily allowance of cholesterol is 300 mg. What is 80% of the recommended daily allowance of cholesterol?

   _____

Name _____ **Date** _____

Remembering

1. It takes Jeff 14 minutes to drive $10\frac{1}{2}$ miles. At this rate, how many minutes will it take him to drive 23 miles?

_____

Solve.

2. $56.3 - 19.34$

_____

3. $116 \div 29$

_____

4. $34.95 \div 1.5$

_____

5. $\frac{1}{2} \div 1\frac{2}{3}$

_____

6. $3\frac{4}{5} + 2\frac{1}{3}$

_____

7. $4\frac{5}{7} \div 2\frac{3}{4}$

_____

Solve.

8. What is 56% of 500 pages?

_____

9. 256 is 40% of what number?

_____

10. Joy drank 48 ounces of water. This was 80% of the total amount of water in the pitcher. How much water was in the pitcher?

_____

11. Indi bought a shirt for $30. He paid 7% sales tax. How much sales tax did Indi pay?

_____

12. **Stretch Your Thinking** Jonah took a survey. Of the students he surveyed, 40% of the students play baseball. Of those students, 60% also play soccer. If 12 students play both baseball and soccer, how many students did Jonah survey? Explain.

_____

_____

_____

_____

Solve Percent Problems

1. Write two unit rates relating meters (m) and kilometers (km).

   _____

2. Convert 525 m to km using any method.

   525 m = _____ km

3. Convert 4.3 km to m using any method.

   4.3 km = _____ m

4. There are 5,280 feet in 1 mile. Write two unit rates relating feet (ft) and miles (mi).

   _____

5. Convert 26,400 feet to miles.

   26,400 ft = _____ mi

6. Convert $\frac{3}{4}$ mile to feet.

   $\frac{3}{4}$ mi = _____ ft

Solve.

7. Find the area of a right triangle with base length 30 inches and height 3 feet.

   _____

8. A cart is 50 cm tall. The cart has three boxes stacked on it, each 40 cm tall. Will the cart and the boxes fit through a door 2 m tall? Explain.

   _____

   _____

9. The soccer field is 300 feet long and 150 feet wide. The coach asked the players to run around the perimeter of the field 20 times during practice. One player commented that they must have run at least 5 miles. Was she right? Explain.

   _____

   _____

   _____

Remembering

1. A bag of dried fruit is made up of 6 parts dried cranberries and 7 parts dried apricots. How many ounces of each fruit would be in a 117-ounce bag?

_____

2. The equation below shows the cost of markers. In the equation, m is the number of markers purchased and c is the cost of the markers in dollars. Complete the table.

$$c = 0.75m$$

Number of Markers (m)	Cost in Dollars (c)
1	
2	
3	
4	

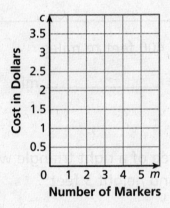

Cost in Dollars

3.5
3
2.5
2
1.5
1
0.5

0 1 2 3 4 5 m
Number of Markers

3. Plot the points from the table. Connect the points if it makes sense to do so.

4. In Jill's class, there are 25 students and 14 of them are in the play. In Hiro's class there are 32 students and 24 of them are in the play. Which class has the greater percentage of students in the play?

_____

5. **Stretch Your Thinking** Vinny adds $136 + 17$ and decides that 34% of 453 is greater than 153. Explain Vinny's thinking.

_____

_____

_____

Homework

Solve.

Show your work.

1. The gas tank on a scooter holds 8.4 L of gas. How many milliliters is this?

   _____

2. A road race will have 7,500 runners. The race organizers want to have 500 mL of water available for each runner. How many liters of water will they need?

   _____

3. Samantha has a 15-gallon fish tank. She is filling it using a 1-quart container.

   a. How many times will she have to fill the container to completely fill the tank?

      _____

   b. If Samantha uses a 1-pint container instead of a 1-quart container, how many times will she have to fill it?

      _____

4. During this track season, Mario has run five 1,500-meter races and three 3,000-meter races. How many kilometers has he run in these eight races combined?

   _____

5. A puppy weighs 6 pounds. If he gains 12 ounces a week for the next 9 weeks, how much will he weigh 9 weeks from now?

   _____

6. A ceramics teacher bought 80 kg of clay and divided it evenly among her 25 students. How many grams of clay did each student get?

   _____

Remembering

1. To make Apple Green paint, Judith combines 5 parts yellow with 2 parts blue. How many gallons of blue does Judith need to use to make 17 gallons of Apple Green paint?

_____

Write three solutions to each inequality.

2. $8 \cdot v < 72$

3. $6 + h > 25$

4. $24 \le \frac{g}{8}$

5. $31 \le k - 31$

Solve.

6. Stuban uses 5 cups walnuts for every 4 cups fruit in his mix. Geraldine uses 8 cups walnuts for every 5 cups fruit. Whose mix will taste nuttier?

7. Pam read 135 pages of a book this week. If this is 45% of the number of pages she normally reads in a week, how many pages does Pam usually read in a week?

8. Barry buys a rug that is 35 inches by 4 feet. What is the area of the rug? Write the answer in square inches and square feet. Then explain your answer.

9. Paul is stacking boxes against a wall that is 3.5 meters high. He has two boxes, one 170 centimeters high and one 134 centimeters high. Can Paul stack the boxes on top of one another? Explain.

10. **Stretch Your Thinking** How many cubic inches are in 1 cubic foot? Explain.

_____

_____

Convert Units of Liquid Volume, Mass, and Weight

Homework

The bar graph and circle graph show data about the
sandwiches sold at Sandwich Stop last Saturday.

Kinds of Sandwiches Sold

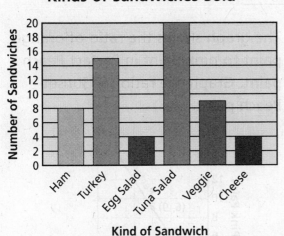

Choice of Bread

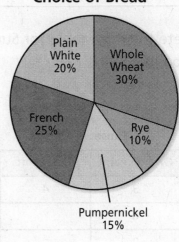

**Solve. Write whether you used the bar graph, the circle
graph, or both.**

1. What percent of the sandwiches were turkey sandwiches?

_____   _____

2. Were more or fewer than $\frac{1}{4}$ of the sandwiches sold made
   on whole wheat bread?

_____   _____

3. How many sandwiches were made using whole
   wheat bread?

_____   _____

4. How many sandwiches were made using French bread?

_____   _____

5. What was the ratio of egg salad sandwiches to tuna
   salad sandwiches?

_____   _____

6. Do the tuna salad sandwiches sold make up more or
   fewer than 25% of the sandwiches sold?

_____   _____

Name _____ **Date** _____

Remembering

1. A light blinks 18 times in 4 minutes. At that rate how many times will it blink in 6 minutes?

_____

2. Complete the ratio table for Sunset Peach paint.

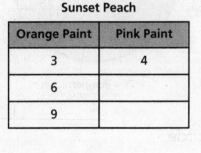

Sunset Peach

Orange Paint	Pink Paint
3	4
6	
9	

3. The graph shows the ratio of orange paint to pink paint in Perfect Peach paint. Graph the ratio for Sunset Peach paint.

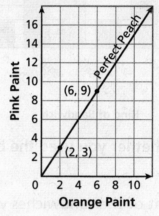

4. Explain how to use the graph to decide which paint is pinker.

_____

_____

_____

Solve.

4. Yolanda pours a pint of juice into each bottle. How many quarts of juice does Yolanda need to fill 90 bottles?

_____

5. Mrs. Houston puts 5 ounces of snack mix in each bag. How many pounds of snack mix does she need to fill 32 bags?

_____

6. **Stretch Your Thinking** An average person may drink 182.5 gallons of water a year. How many cups of water is that? Use the table to help you.

_____

1 pint = 2 cups
1 quart = 2 pints
1 gallon = 4 quarts

Focus on Mathematical Practices

Name _____ **Date** _____

Homework

The tables show 14 students and the number of siblings each student has. A sibling is a brother or sister.

Student	Number of Siblings	Student	Number of Siblings
Maria	2	Daisha	3
Gabe	0	Juan	2
Kwan	1	Yuriko	0
Tyrese	1	Ariana	4
Jose	2	Jiao	2
Sierra	3	Hannah	1
Colton	1	Santiago	3

The dot plot below displays the sibling data from the tables above. Use the dot plot for Exercises 1–3.

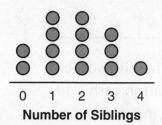

0   1   2   3   4
Number of Siblings

1. What does each dot in the plot represent?

   _____

   _____

2. Does the dot plot correctly display the data in the table? Explain why or why not.

   _____

   _____

   _____

3. Which dot in the plot represents Ariana? Explain.

   _____

   _____

   _____

Remembering

1. A cereal box is 2 in. by 7 in. by 12 in. The box is 75% filled with cereal. What is the volume of the cereal in the box?

_____

Solve the equation.

2. $12 \cdot v = 10$

   $v =$ _____

3. $15 + h = 16$

   $h =$ _____

4. $12 = \frac{a}{8}$

   $a =$ _____

5. $112 = b - 23$

   $b =$ _____

Solve.

6. Jay rode his bicycle 10 blocks. This is 40% of the way from his home to school. How many blocks is it from Jay's home to school?

_____

7. Mrs. Martin is buying a new dishwasher. The dishwasher costs $350. Mrs. Martin pays 35% of the cost in cash and finances the rest. How much does she pay in cash?

_____

8. Cathy is using ribbon to make a border for a rectangular picture frame. The frame is 8 in. by 14 in. Cathy wraps the ribbon around the frame 5 times. Is 6 yards enough ribbon for Cathy to complete the border? Why or why not?

_____

_____

9. **Stretch Your Thinking** Monique drew a dot plot that showed the number of hours of homework 12 of her friends do a day. She says her dot plot shows that all of her friends do the same number of hours of homework. What does her dot plot look like? Explain.

_____

_____

Making Sense of Data

Homework

1. On the grid at the right, draw a dot plot to represent the set of numbers shown below.

   {4, 1, 5, 2, 3, 2, 5, 1, 4, 5, 4, 2, 5, 2, 1}

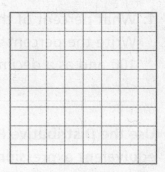

2. The table below shows the daily sales for a pretzel stand during its first 2 weeks. Group the data and then draw and label a histogram of the groups on the grid below the table.

Sales at a Pretzel Stand	
Day	Sales (dollars)
1	971
2	1,227
3	1,018
4	1,050
5	1,148
6	961
7	1,483
8	1,000
9	1,250
10	1,140
11	1,380
12	1,165
13	984
14	1,483

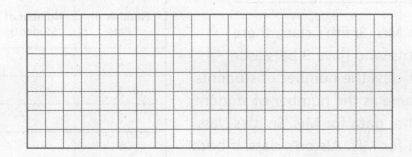

Name _____ **Date** _____

Remembering

1. What percent of the figure at the right is shaded? Write the percent as a fraction with denominator 100 and as a decimal.

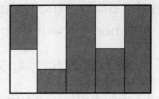

_____

Use the Distributive Property to write an equivalent expression.

2. $6(9t + 5) + s$

_____

3. $4 + 45t + 36t^2 - 2s$

_____

4. $st + 2s^2 + 16s + t^2$

_____

5. $5 + 4s(3t + 2s - 5)$

_____

The dot plot shows the number of pets that students in Mrs. Alston's class have. Use the dot plot for Exercises 6–9.

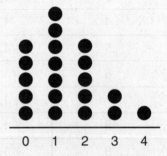

Number of Pets of Students in Mrs. Alston's Class

6. How many students have 2 pets? How do you know?

_____

7. How many more students have 1 pet than have 3 pets?

_____

8. How many students are in Mrs. Alston's class? How do you know?

_____

9. **Stretch Your Thinking** In Mrs. Smith's class, there are twice as many students who have 3 pets as in Mrs. Alston's class. In her class the number of students who have 0 pets is the same as the number of students who have 4 pets. The other data for Mrs. Smith's class are the same as the data for Mrs. Alston's class. If both classes have the same number of students, fill in the chart to show the data for Mrs. Smith's class.

Data for Mrs. Smith's Class	
Number of Pets	Number of Students
0	
1	
2	
3	
4	

Dot Plots and Histograms

Homework

Use the four groups of cubes below for Exercises 1 and 2.

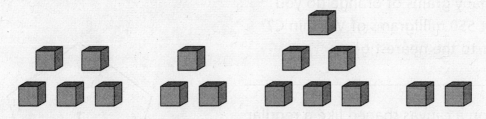

1. Explain what the phrase *leveling out to form fair shares* means.

   _____

   _____

   _____

2. Explain how to level out the groups
   shown above so that each group
   represents a fair share. Use the words
   add and *subtract* in your answer. Then
   sketch the fair shares in the space at the right.

   _____

   _____

   _____

**The data table at the right shows the number of goals
the members of a soccer team scored last season.
Use the data for Exercises 3 and 4.**

Player	Number of Goals Scored
Owen	3
Jermichael	10
Ryder	0
Aziz	6
Liam	14
Stephon	1
Ollie	4
Tyson	1
Hudson	11
Ray	0

3. Explain how to find the mean number of goals
   scored by the players.

   _____

   _____

   _____

4. Find the mean number of goals scored by completing the
   number sentence below.

   _____ ÷ _____ = _____

Remembering

1. There are 53 milligrams of Vitamin C in 100 grams of orange. How many grams of orange do you need to eat to get 550 milligrams of Vitamin C? Round the answer to the nearest gram.

   _____

2. Cindy is painting on a canvas shaped like a regular pentagon as shown. She covers $\frac{4}{5}$ of the canvas with paint. How much of the canvas is covered in paint?

   _____

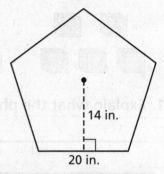

14 in.

20 in.

The table shows the ages of the actors in a school play. Use the data for Exercises 3–4.

3. Group the data. Then, on the grid below, draw and label a histogram of the data.

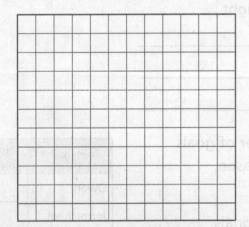

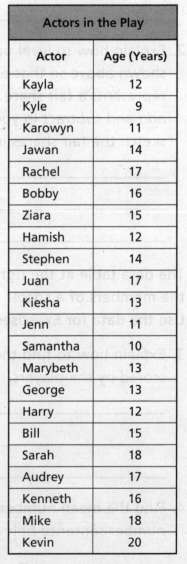

Actors in the Play	
Actor	**Age (Years)**
Kayla	12
Kyle	9
Karowyn	11
Jawan	14
Rachel	17
Bobby	16
Ziara	15
Hamish	12
Stephen	14
Juan	17
Kiesha	13
Jenn	11
Samantha	10
Marybeth	13
George	13
Harry	12
Bill	15
Sarah	18
Audrey	17
Kenneth	16
Mike	18
Kevin	20

4. **Stretch Your Thinking** What percent of the actors in the play are younger than 17 years old? Round the answer to the nearest percent. Explain.

   _____

   _____

Homework

Solve.

1. In Mr. Jackson's language arts class,
   the mean of nine weekly test scores
   determines the quarterly grade.

Eight of Latoya's Nine Weekly Scores
100 96 90 95 95 100 88 98

   a. What is the sum of Latoya's eight scores?

   _____

   b. What must the sum of Latoya's *nine* scores be
      for her to earn an average test score of 95?
      Explain your answer.

   _____

   _____

   c. What is the minimum score Latoya must earn on the
      final test to have an average test score of 95 for the
      quarter? Explain your answer.

   _____

   _____

Use the table for Exercises 2 and 3.

The number of students enrolled at two middle schools
is shown in the table at the right. Ford School has one
class at each grade level. Carter School has two classes
at each grade level.

Middle School Enrollment		
Grade	Ford School	Carter School
6	21	41
7	19	36
8	20	37

2. Using words, explain how to find the average
   number of students per class at each school.

   _____

   _____

3. Calculate the mean number of students per class at
   each school. Write your answers in sentences that
   explain what the means represent.

   _____

   _____

Name _____ **Date** _____

Remembering

Solve.

1. Valerie mixes 5 parts liquid fertilizer for every 9 parts water to make fertilizer for her garden. How many quarts of water and fertilizer does she need to make 20 quarts of solution?

   _____

   _____

2. What percent is 45 of 125?

   _____

Write equivalent fractions. Complete.

3.	$3\frac{5}{6}$ $3\frac{3}{8}$ →	
4.	>, <	
5.	+	
6.	•	
7.	÷	
8.	−	

Complete the number sentence to find the mean of each data set.

9. 3, 4, 7, 4, 2, 4, 6, 2

   _____ ÷ _____ = _____

10. 10, 11, 12, 11, 11

   _____ ÷ _____ = _____

11. 9, 14, 10, 0, 0, 4, 10, 7, 9

   _____ ÷ _____ = _____

12. 20, 23, 35, 14

   _____ ÷ _____ = _____

Use the histogram for Exercises 13–14.

13. The 0 to 4 age group has $\frac{2}{3}$ as many people as which other group?

   _____

14. **Stretch Your Thinking** What is the mean number of people in each age range? Explain.

   _____

   _____

   _____

   _____

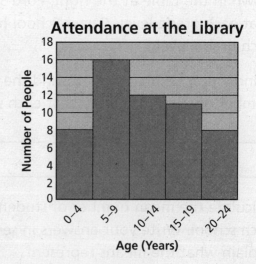

Attendance at the Library

Number of People / Age (Years)

Use the Mean

Homework

Draw a dot plot to show the new arrangement of dots.

1. Move one dot to the left and move one
   dot to the right so the balance point
   remains the same.

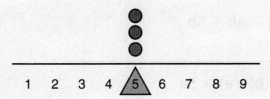

2. Move all of the dots so the balance point
   remains the same.

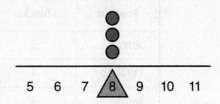

3. Move all of the dots so the balance point
   changes to a lesser whole number. Draw
   the new balance point.

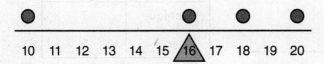

4. Move all of the dots so the balance point
   changes to a greater whole number. Draw
   the new balance point.

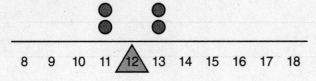

Remembering

1. The ratio of width to length of a TV screen is 4 to 5. What is the area of a TV screen with width 30 inches?

   _____

Evaluate for $a = 1.2$ and $b = 4$.

2. $b^2 + a(4 + b)$

   _____

3. $45 - ab + 5b$

   _____

4. $5 + a + b + 4ab$

   _____

5. $16(b - a) - 5a$

   _____

6. Draw a dot plot to represent the data in the table. Title your display.

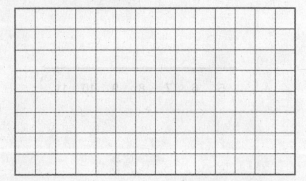

Blocks Students Walk to School	
Student	**Blocks**
Jerry	2
Luciano	4
Jaime	3
Austin	4
Zubia	5
Tasmina	2
Julian	4
Monique	7
Cheryl	5

7. Nancy got an 88, 95, 87, 100, and 90 on her tests. What does she need to get on her next test to have an average of 93?

   _____

8. **Stretch Your Thinking** The average number of people at a concert over 3 nights is 125. On the first night, there were 151 people at the concert. The same number of people attended on the second and third nights. How many people attended on each of the second and third nights? Explain.

   _____

   _____

   _____

Homework

Solve.

1. The dot plot at the right displays 11 data values. Find the median of the data.

_____

```
    ○     ○
    ○     ○          ○
    ○     ○          ○     ○
    ○     ○    ○     ○     ○
   15   16   17   18   19   20
```

The table at the right shows the number of students in each grade who volunteered to be in the talent show. Use the table for Exercises 2 and 3.

2. What is the median number of volunteers for each grade?

_____

3. Did Grade 6 have more volunteers than the median number of volunteers? Explain.

_____

_____

Grade	Number of Volunteers
1	30
2	9
3	40
4	32
5	41
6	29
7	30
8	35

The number of minutes William studied at home each school night for two weeks is shown in the table at the right. Use the table for Exercises 4–6.

4. Calculate the mean number of minutes for each week.

   Week 1 mean: _____   Week 2 mean: _____

5. Calculate the median number of minutes for each week.

   Week 1 median: _____   Week 2 median: _____

6. Suppose William wants to summarize the data for both weeks using only one number. What number should he choose? Give a reason to support your answer.

_____

_____

Minutes	
Week 1	Week 2
10	0
30	10
10	15
10	10
0	0

Remembering

1. When Michelle practices her instrument, she spends 8 minutes practicing songs and 5 minutes practicing scales. How long does Michelle need to practice to spend 16 minutes practicing songs?

_____

Draw a dot plot to show the new arrangement of dots.

2. Move all of the dots so the balance point remains the same.

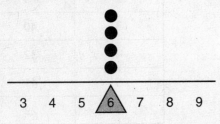

    3   4   5   6   7   8   9   3   4   5   6   7   8   9

3. Move all of the dots so the balance point changes to a greater whole number. Draw the new balance point.

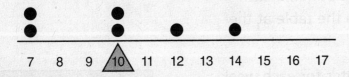

    7   8   9   10   11   12   13   14   15   16   17

    7   8   9   10   11   12   13   14   15   16   17

4. **Stretch Your Thinking** The balance point of a set of 4 numbers is 14. How can you move one point to make the balance point 16? Explain.

_____

_____

_____

Find and Use the Median

1. The youngest child in a family is 6 years old. The oldest parent is 35 years old. What is the range of ages in the family?

_____

2. Will every family have the same range of ages as the family in Exercise 1? Explain why or why not.

_____

_____

3. Quartiles divide a set of data into how many equal parts?

_____

Use the set of data at the right for Exercises 4–6.

4. Label the median.

5. Label the first quartile.

6. Label the third quartile.

73
102
319
565
570
844
1,096

Use the dot plots below for Exercises 7 and 8.

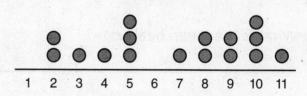

7. Plot A: range: _____

   median: _____

   first quartile: _____

   third quartile: _____

8. Plot B: range: _____

   median: _____

   first quartile: _____

   third quartile: _____

Remembering

1. Tayshawn is going to spend 35% of his money on a gift for his mother. If the gift costs $42, how much money does Tayshawn have?

_____

The table shows the average heart rate for different animals, including humans. Use the data for Exercises 2–4.

2. Group the data. Then draw and label a histogram of the data on the grid below.

Animal	Average Heart Rate (beats per minute)
Human	60
Medium dog	90
Horse	44
Cow	65
Pig	70
Elephant	30
Giraffe	65
Large whale	20
Small dog	100
Large dog	75

3. What is the mean heart rate?

_____

4. What is the median heart rate?

_____

5. **Stretch Your Thinking** The median of a set of data is $\frac{2}{3}$ of the greatest value and $1\frac{2}{5}$ of the least value. The data set has 7 numbers that are all whole numbers. The mean of the data set is equal to the median. What could be the values in the data set?

_____

Variability in Data

1. Make a box plot to represent the dot plot data.

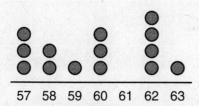

57 58 59 60 61 62 63   57 58 59 60 61 62 63

Three summaries of data displayed by a box plot are shown at the right. Use the summaries for Exercise 2.

Q1 = 0.75
median = 5.5
Q3 = 6.25

2. How does the range from the median to Q1 compare to the range from the median to Q3, and what does this suggest about the spread of the data?

_____

_____

_____

_____

Use the box plots below for Exercises 3–5.

Box Plot A

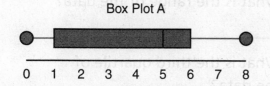

0 1 2 3 4 5 6 7 8

Box Plot B

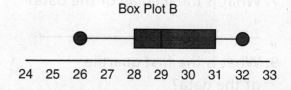

24 25 26 27 28 29 30 31 32 33

3. Calculate the IQR of Box Plot A.   4. Calculate the IQR of Box Plot B.

_____   _____

5. Which IQR is a better description of the spread or dispersion of the data? Give a reason to support your answer.

_____

_____

_____

_____

Remembering

1. Jadzia finished 8 of the 10 problems she had for homework. What percent of her homework did Jadzia finish?

   _____

Solve for k.

2. $\frac{k}{24} = \frac{12}{80}$

   k = _____

3. $\frac{23}{13} = \frac{k}{34}$

   k = _____

4. $\frac{15}{k} = \frac{3}{20}$

   k = _____

The dot plot shows the number of feet of ribbon used for a project by students in Mr. Del Rio's class. Use the dot plot for Exercises 5–11.

5. How many students used more than 15 feet of ribbon?

   _____

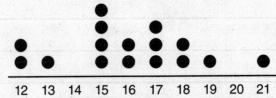

Feet of Ribbon Used for Project

6. What is the mean of the data?

   _____

7. What is the median of the data?

   _____

8. What is the range of the data?

   _____

9. What is the first quartile of the data?

   _____

10. What is the third quartile of the data?

   _____

11. **Stretch Your Thinking** Suppose data values for 3 more students are added to the dot plot above. The students used 19, 20, and 21 feet of ribbon. How would the new data affect the median, first quartile, and third quartile values?

   _____

   _____

   _____

Homework

Use the dot plot below for Exercises 1–4.

The Mean of These Values is 5   Distance from the Mean

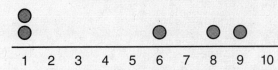

| 1 | 2 | 3 | 4 | 5 | 6 | 7 | 8 | 9 | 10 |

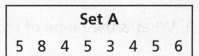

| 1 | 2 | 3 | 4 | 5 | 6 | 7 | 8 | 9 | 10 |

1. Complete the *Distance from the Mean* display by writing a number to represent each dot's distance from the mean.

2. Find the sum of the distances from the mean.

_____

3. Divide the sum of the distances by the number of values.

_____

4. What does the answer to Exercise 3 represent?

_____

Follow the steps below to calculate the mean absolute deviation of the data in Set A, shown at the right.

Set A
5 8 4 5 3 4 5 6

5. Find the mean of the data. _____

6. Find the distance each value is from the mean.

_____

_____

7. Write the sum of the distances. _____

8. Calculate the mean absolute deviation by dividing the sum of the distances by the number of values.

_____

9. In Exercise 8, you calculated the mean absolute deviation of the data in Set A. Suppose the mean absolute deviation of a different set of data called Set B was double your answer for Exercise 8. How would the spread of data in the two sets compare?

_____

_____

Remembering

1. A honey mustard sauce recipe calls for 1 part mustard and 2 parts honey. How much of each ingredient is needed to make 12 cups of sauce?

_____

Use the data in the table for Exercises 2–8.

2. Draw a dot plot to represent the data in the table. Title your display.

Food Donations			
Grade	Number of Cans	Grade	Number of Cans
1	28	7	28
2	30	8	25
3	23	9	29
4	23	10	20
5	20	11	29
6	30	12	29

3. What is the range of the data?

_____

4. What is the median of the data?

_____

5. What is the first quartile of the data?

_____

6. What is the third quartile of the data?

_____

7. Make a box plot to represent the data.

20　21　22　23　24　25　26　27　28　29　30

8. **Stretch Your Thinking** Calculate the IQR of the box plot above. Is the IQR a good description of the data? Why or why not?

_____

_____

_____

Mean Absolute Deviation

Homework

Use the dot plot below for Exercises 1–4.

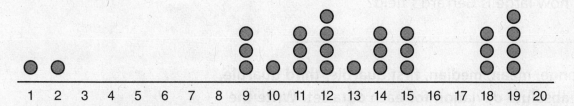

1. Describe the shape of the data. Use the words *clusters*, *peaks*, *gaps*, and *outliers* in your answer.

_____

_____

_____

_____

2. The dot at 13 is the median of the data. Would the median change if it was calculated a second time without including the values at 1 and 2? Explain why or why not.

_____

_____

_____

3. The mean of the data is 13. Would the mean change if it was calculated a second time without including the values at 1 and 2? Explain why or why not.

_____

_____

_____

4. Which measure, mean or median, best describes the set of data? Give a reason to support your answer.

_____

_____

_____

Remembering

1. Gerrard mowed 25% of his field. If he mowed 2 acres, how large is Gerrard's field?

_____

Find the range, mean, median, first quartile, third quartile, and mean absolute deviation for each data set. Write the answer as a decimal to the nearest tenth when necessary.

2. 5, 4, 2, 3, 7, 9

   range: _____

   mean: _____

   median: _____

   first quartile: _____

   third quartile: _____

   mean absolute deviation: _____

3. 66, 65, 67, 50, 54, 56, 69

   range: _____

   mean: _____

   median: _____

   first quartile: _____

   third quartile: _____

   mean absolute deviation: _____

4. 8, 11, 14, 7, 12, 12, 12, 20

   range: _____

   mean: _____

   median: _____

   first quartile: _____

   third quartile: _____

   mean absolute deviation: _____

5. 4, 3, 5, 2, 4, 4, 6

   range: _____

   mean: _____

   median: _____

   first quartile: _____

   third quartile: _____

   mean absolute deviation: _____

6. **Stretch Your Thinking** Look at your answers for Exercises 2–5. Which data set is most spread out? Explain.

_____

_____

_____

Clusters, Peaks, Gaps, and Outliers

A sixth grade class built and flew paper airplanes. The data collected by the class are shown in the dot plot below.

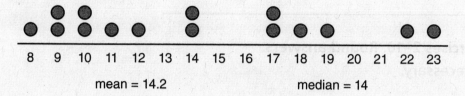

8 9 10 11 12 13 14 15 16 17 18 19 20 21 22 23

mean = 14.2   median = 14

Build and fly a paper airplane at home. A family member may have an interesting design idea for you to try. Fly the plane several times and record the greatest distance it flies in feet.

Remember! Paper airplanes can cause injuries, so fly your plane in a safe manner.

1. How does the greatest distance your plane flew compare to the mean and median of the dot plot above?

   _____

   _____

Suppose you drew a new dot on the plot to represent the distance your plane flew. Will the new dot:

2. become part of a cluster? _____

3. become part of a peak? _____

4. create a different gap in the data? _____

5. be an outlier? _____

6. Predict how the new dot will affect the mean and the median of the data. Explain your predictions.

   _____

   _____

   _____

   _____

Name _____ **Date** _____

Remembering

1. It takes Stephen 15 minutes to travel 45 blocks on his bicycle. At this rate, how far can he travel in 45 minutes?

   _____

Use the dot plot for Exercises 2–10. Round answers to the nearest tenth if necessary.

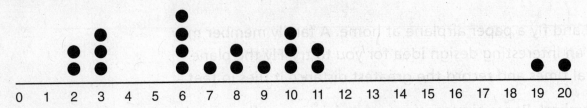

2. range: _____

3. mean: _____

4. median: _____

5. mean absolute deviation: _____

6. first quartile: _____

7. third quartile: _____

8. Describe the shape of the data. Use the words *clusters*, *peaks*, *gaps*, and *outliers* in your answer.

   _____

   _____

9. Make a box plot to represent the dot plot data.

   _____

   0 1 2 3 4 5 6 7 8 9 10 11 12 13 14 15 16 17 18 19 20

10. **Stretch Your Thinking** How would your answers in Exercises 2–9 be affected if they were calculated without the values at 19 and 20? Explain.

    _____

    _____

    _____

    _____

Collect, Display, and Interpret Data

Homework

In a previous activity, you estimated the area of one of your hands. How might the area of one of your feet compare to the area of your hand?

1. **Predict** Complete the sentence below by writing the phrase *greater than, less than,* or *the same as.*

   I predict that the area of my foot is _____ the area of my hand.

2. Look back at Activity 1 and find your estimate of the area of your hand.

   The area of my hand is about _____ square centimeters.

3. **Predict** What do you think the area of your foot might be? Record your prediction in square centimeters.

   _____

4. Trace one of your feet on centimeter grid paper.

5. Estimate the area of your foot by counting whole and partial square centimeters. What is your estimate of the area?

   _____

6. **Compare** How does the area of your foot compare to the area of your hand?

   _____

   _____

7. What percent, rounded to the nearest whole, is the area of your foot when compared to the area of your hand?

   _____

Remembering

1. Nathaniel has a number cube with a side length of
   1 cm. Bonnie has a different number cube with a
   side length of 2 cm. What percent of the surface area
   of Bonnie's cube is the surface area of Nathaniel's cube?

   _____

Solve.

2. $234.6 \div 3.4$

3. $0.021 \cdot 0.45$

4. $12{,}098 - 9{,}993$

   _____   _____   _____

Use the data set at the right for Exercises 5–7.

| 12 | 12 | 13 | 11 | 10 | 19 | 19 | 21 | 22 |

5. Draw a dot plot to represent the data.

   10 11 12 13 14 15 16 17 18 19 20 21 22

6. Make a box plot to represent the data.

   10 11 12 13 14 15 16 17 18 19 20 21 22

7. **Stretch Your Thinking** Add a new data value to
   the data set that would change the box plot.
   Explain how the box plot would change.

   _____

   _____

   _____

Focus on Mathematical Practices

Homework

Many real world situations involve numbers that are less than zero. For example, the thermometer activity you completed involved some temperatures that were less than zero.

For each real world situation below, write the *opposite* situation.

1. 3,000 feet above sea level _____

2. $45 savings account withdrawal _____

3. 9 positive electrical charges _____

4. $488 checking account deposit _____

5. 1 foot below sea level _____

Solve.

6. The solar panels on the Jordan's home generate electricity. During the month of August, the Jordan family used 570 kilowatt hours of electricity. If their electric bill for August was $0.00, what amount of electricity did they generate that month?

_____

Each arrow on the Fahrenheit thermometer points to a temperature. Write the temperature, and then write the *opposite* temperature.

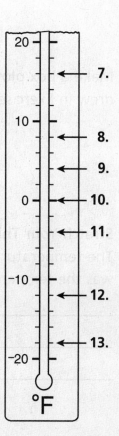

7. _____

8. _____

9. _____

10. _____

11. _____

12. _____

13. _____

Remembering

1. Jaquilynn's goal is to save $120. She has saved 40% of this. How much money has she saved?

_____

Give three solutions to each inequality.

2. $8 < 6 + t$

_____

3. $5 \cdot b \leq 28$

_____

4. $36 > \frac{s}{4}$

_____

5. $e - 22 \geq 29$

_____

Solve.

6. Draw a dot plot that has 2 peaks, 2 clusters, 1 gap, a median of 16, and a range of 12.

7. Make a box plot to represent the dot plot data you drew in Exercise 6.

8. **Stretch Your Thinking** In the afternoon, it was 12°F. The temperature dropped 15°F in the evening. What was the temperature in the evening? Explain.

_____

_____

_____

Negative Numbers in the Real World

Name   **Date**

Homework

Solve.

1. What integer represents the origin of a number line? _____

2. Suppose a point is located 12 unit lengths below the origin of a vertical number line. What integer represents the point? _____

3. On a horizontal number line, a point is located at ⁺15. Describe the *distance* and *direction* of the point.

_____

_____

Use the number line at the right for Exercises 4–6.

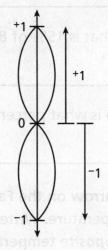

4. What do the loops on the number line show?

_____

5. How do the arrows for ⁺1 and ⁻1 show both *distance* and *direction*?

_____

_____

6. Are ⁺1 and ⁻1 opposite integers? Explain.

_____

_____

_____

7. On the number line below, draw a point at each tick mark, and label each point with an integer.

Remembering

Solve.

1. Passion Fruit purple paint is made from 7 parts red and 3 parts blue. How many gallons of red do you need to use to make 15 gallons of Passion Fruit purple paint?

_____

2. Mr. Kolb is putting hard wood flooring in the area of his house shown at the right. He is also putting crown molding around the edge of the area. How much flooring does Mr. Kolb need? How much molding?

_____

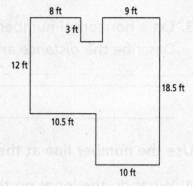

3. What is 15% of 80?

_____

4. 32% of what number is 112?

_____

5. 70 is what percent of 350?

_____

6. 95% of what number is 285?

_____

Each arrow on the Fahrenheit thermometer points to a temperature. Write the temperature, and then write the _opposite_ temperature.

7. _____

8. _____

9. _____

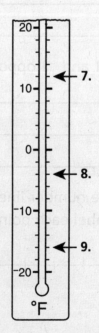

10. **Stretch Your Thinking** The temperature is 16°F cooler in the morning than in the afternoon. If it is 9°F below zero in the morning, what is the temperature in the afternoon? Explain.

_____

_____

Integers on a Number Line

Name _____ **Date** _____

Homework

Compare. Write <, >, or =.

‹—┼—›
⁻10 ⁻9 ⁻8 ⁻7 ⁻6 ⁻5 ⁻4 ⁻3 ⁻2 ⁻1 0 1 2 3 4 5 6 7 8 9 10

1. ⁻3 ◯ ⁻5   **2.** ⁻7 ◯ ⁻1   **3.** 2 ◯ 9   **4.** 1 ◯ ⁻6

5. ⁻2 ◯ 0   **6.** ⁻4 ◯ ⁻8   **7.** ⁻6 ◯ ⁻5   **8.** 0 ◯ ⁻4

9. ⁻1 ◯ 6   **10.** ⁻3 ◯ ⁻2   **11.** ⁻8 ◯ ⁻8   **12.** ⁻3 ◯ ⁻9

Write the numbers in order from _least_ to _greatest_.

13. ⁻3, 0, ⁻4 _____   **14.** ⁻6, ⁻7, ⁻5 _____

Write the numbers in order from _greatest_ to _least_.

15. 0, ⁻2, 1, ⁻1 _____   **16.** ⁻3, 0, ⁻8, 3 _____

Use absolute value to compare the numbers.
Then write <, >, or =.

17. ⁻6 ◯ ⁻1   **18.** ⁻2 ◯ ⁻5   **19.** ⁻4 ◯ ⁻9   **20.** ⁻7 ◯ ⁻3

Solve. Use the situation below for Exercises 21 and 22.

On a Tuesday night during February in Brainerd, Minnesota,
the low temperature was ⁻7°F. On the next night, the low
temperature was ⁻4°F.

21. Explain how absolute value can be used to find the
warmer low temperature. Then name the temperature.

_____

_____

22. Explain how a number line can be used to find the
colder low temperature. Then name the temperature.

_____

_____

_____

Name _____ **Date** _____

Remembering

Solve.

1. At a used book sale, all books are the same price. Jeff buys 15 books for $12. How much would 40 books cost?

   _____

2. How many cubic yards of topsoil will be used to cover a 10 yard by 12 yard playground if the topsoil is 24 inches deep?

   _____

3. Belinda used 85% of the pieces of wood that she had to build a bird house. If she used 68 pieces of wood, how many pieces of wood did she have in all?

   _____

4. Tommy is filling an 18-gallon aquarium with a 2-quart container. How many times does Tommy need to fill the container to completely fill the tank?

   _____

Write the opposite integer.

5. 7 _____   6. ⁻27 _____   7. ⁻15 _____   8. 5 _____

9. ⁻12 _____   10. 23 _____   11. ⁻8 _____   12. ⁻18 _____

13. Write the value of points *A*, *B*, and *C*.

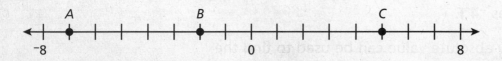

Point *A* _____   Point *B* _____   Point *C* _____

14. **Stretch Your Thinking** Jenna starts at ⁻5 on the number line. She jumps 8 places to the right. Then she jumps 5 places to the left. Where is Jenna on the number line? Explain.

   _____

   _____

Compare and Order Integers

Solve.

1. A point in the coordinate plane is on the *y*-axis and 8 units below the origin. What ordered pair represents the point? Explain your answer.

_____

_____

_____

2. The signs of the coordinates of an ordered pair are $(+, -)$. In which quadrant is the point located? Explain your answer.

_____

_____

_____

Use the coordinate plane below for Exercises 3–10.

Write the location of each point.

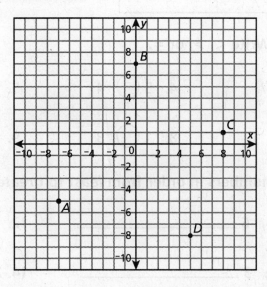

3. Point *A* _____

4. Point *B* _____

5. Point *C* _____

6. Point *D* _____

Plot and label each point.

7. Point *W* at (⁻3, 0)

8. Point *X* at (6, ⁻2)

9. Point *Y* at (⁻4, ⁻10)

10. Point *Z* at (⁻6, 6)

Remembering

Solve.

Stefan is buying books at the book fair. There is a $3 fee to enter the fair. Each book costs $0.75. Use this information for Exercises 1–2.

1. Write an equation that can be used to find the total cost in dollars, c, of buying b books.

   _____

2. Use your equation to complete the table.

books, b	cost of books, c
1	
2	
3	
4	
5	

Compare. Write <, >, or =.

3. 8 ◯ ⁻7   4. ⁻5 ◯ ⁻4   5. ⁻10 ◯ 10   6. ⁻9 ◯ ⁻9

7. 11 ◯ ⁻1   8. ⁻1 ◯ ⁻3   9. ⁻5 ◯ 4   10. ⁻5 ◯ ⁻9

Write the numbers in order from *least* to *greatest*.

11. 4, 9, ⁻4, ⁻6 _____   12. ⁻9, ⁻11, ⁻1, 2 _____

13. 0, 9, 5, ⁻3 _____   14. 2, ⁻3, ⁻4, ⁻6 _____

15. **Stretch Your Thinking** Gina, Sam, Tony, and Beth all have numbers. Gina's number is between Tony's and Beth's. Beth's number is the only one that is not negative. Sam's number is to the left of Tony's on the number line. If the numbers are 5, ⁻3, ⁻5, and ⁻6, which number belongs to which person?

_____

Name _____ **Date** _____

Homework

Use the number line at the right for Exercises 1–7.

1. What place value does the number line show?
   Explain how you know.

   _____

   _____

2. Label each tick mark to the right of the number line
   with a decimal.

3. Label each tick mark to the left of the number line with
   a fraction in simplest form.

4. Draw a point at 0.2. Label it *W*.

5. Draw a point at $\frac{-7}{10}$. Label it *Z*.

6. Draw a point at $\frac{4}{5}$. Label it *Y*.

7. Draw a point at $^-0.9$. Label it *X*.

Solve.

8. On a number line, the rational number $\frac{-9}{4}$ is located to the
   left of zero. The rational number $2\frac{1}{4}$ is located to the right of zero.
   Are the numbers opposite rational numbers? Explain.

   _____

   _____

Write the opposite rational number.

9. $\frac{-1}{3}$ _____

10. $\frac{5}{6}$ _____

11. $\frac{-7}{16}$ _____

12. $\frac{3}{10}$ _____

Simplify.

13. $^-(-\frac{1}{3})$ _____

14. $^-(0.75)$ _____

15. $^-(^-0.5)$ _____

16. $^-(\frac{4}{5})$ _____

Remembering

1. Mr. Ruete's dog eats 3 packages of dog treats every 4 weeks. How many packages of dog treats does the dog eat in 10 weeks?

_____

Solve for s.

2. $6s = 100$

$s =$ _____

3. $\frac{s}{6} = 100$

$s =$ _____

4. $44.53 \div 7.3 = s$

$s =$ _____

5. $27 \cdot 12.34 = s$

$s =$ _____

Use the coordinate plane for Exercises 6–13.

Write the location of each point.

6. Point *A*

_____

7. Point *B*

_____

8. Point *C*

_____

9. Point *D*

_____

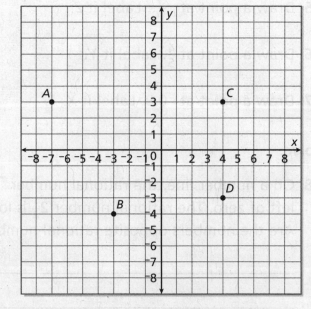

Plot and label each point.

10. Point *E* at (0, ⁻6)

11. Point *F* at (3, ⁻7)

12. Point *G* at (6, ⁻3)

13. Point *H* at (⁻3, 4)

14. **Stretch Your Thinking** Courtney plotted a point (*x*, *y*) where the absolute value of *x* is 2 times the absolute value of *y* and the *x*-value is 18 less than the *y*-value. What point did Courtney plot? Explain.

_____

_____

Rational Numbers on a Number Line

Name _____ **Date** _____

Homework

Solve.

1. Suppose two rational numbers are plotted on a *vertical* number line. Is the number that is below the other number the greater number, or the lesser number?

_____

2. Suppose two rational numbers are plotted on a *horizontal* number line. Is the number farther to the right the greater number, or the lesser number?

_____

Use the number line below for Exercises 3–17.

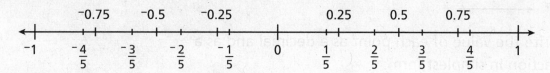

Compare. Write <, >, or =.

3. $\frac{1}{5} \bigcirc \frac{^-2}{5}$

4. $^-0.75 \bigcirc ^-0.5$

5. $0.25 \bigcirc ^-1$

6. $\frac{^-4}{5} \bigcirc \frac{^-3}{5}$

7. $\frac{^-1}{5} \bigcirc ^-0.5$

8. $^-0.25 \bigcirc 0$

9. $\left|^-0.5\right| \bigcirc \left|\frac{^-4}{5}\right|$

10. $^-1 \bigcirc \frac{^-5}{5}$

11. $1 \bigcirc ^-(^-0.75)$

12. $\left|\frac{^-3}{5}\right| \bigcirc \left|\frac{3}{5}\right|$

13. $0 \bigcirc \frac{2}{5}$

14. $\frac{^-2}{5} \bigcirc ^-\left(\frac{^-4}{5}\right)$

Write the numbers in order from *greatest* to *least*.

15. $\frac{^-1}{5}, \frac{4}{5}, \frac{^-3}{5}$

16. $0, ^-0.75, ^-1, ^-0.5$

17. $^-0.25, \frac{2}{5}, 1, \frac{^-4}{5}$

_____   _____   _____

Solve.

18. On Monday morning, a stock began the day trading at $14.11 per share. At midweek, the stock traded at $14.28 per share. At the close of business on Friday, the share price was $13.97.

    Write the share prices in order from least to greatest.

_____

Name _____ **Date** _____

Remembering

1. For every 8 multiple-choice questions on Minnie's math test, there are 5 short-answer questions. How many multiple-choice and short-answer questions are on a test with 65 questions?

_____

Find the missing measure.

2. rectangle

   $w = 4.5\ m$

   $A = 94.5\ m^2$

   $l =$ _____

3. cube

   $SA = 294\ yd^2$

   $s =$ _____

4. octagon

   $P = 121.6\ cm$

   $s =$ _____

5. Write the value of each point as a decimal and as a fraction in simplest form.

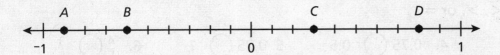

Point A _____   Point B _____

Point C _____   Point D _____

Write the opposite rational number.

6. $\dfrac{-5}{6}$ _____

7. $1\dfrac{3}{5}$ _____

8. $-3\dfrac{1}{4}$ _____

9. $\dfrac{7}{10}$ _____

10. **Stretch Your Thinking** Keyshawn plotted a point halfway between $-\dfrac{1}{2}$ and $-\dfrac{2}{5}$ on the number line. What number does Keyshawn's point represent? Write the number as a fraction in simplest form and as a decimal. Explain.

_____

_____

_____

Compare and Order Rational Numbers

Name _____ **Date** _____

Homework

On the coordinate grid, Points A, B, and C represent
ships at sea. Use the grid for Exercises 1–4.

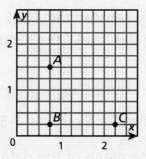

1. Write the location of each point.

   Point A _____

   Point B _____

   Point C _____

2. Explain how subtraction can be used to find the number of unit lengths
   the ship at Point A is from the ship at Point B. Then write the distance.

   _____

   _____

3. Explain how subtraction can be used to find the number of unit lengths
   the ship at Point C is from the ship at point B. Then write the distance.

   _____

   _____

4. The ship at Point B is 300 nautical miles south of the ship at Point A,
   and 360 nautical miles west of the ship at Point C. What number of
   nautical miles does each unit length of the grid represent?

   _____

Solve.

5. Suppose a point at $(5\frac{1}{2}, 6\frac{1}{2})$ is reflected across the y-axis. Explain how
   to find the location of the reflected point, and then write its location.

   _____

   _____

6. Suppose a point at $(^-7.75, 7.25)$ is reflected across the x-axis. Explain how
   to find the location of the reflected point, and then write its location.

   _____

   _____

Remembering

1. It took the Lehman family 25 minutes to crack 60 eggs. How long did it take the family to crack each egg?

_____

Use the dot plot for Exercises 2–5.

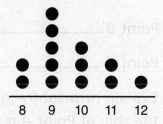

2. What is the mean of the data? Round the answer to the nearest tenth.

_____

3. What is the median of the data?

_____

4. Find the first and third quartiles.

first quartile: _____ third quartile: _____

5. Make a box plot to represent the dot plot data.

_____

8   9   10   11   12

Compare. Write <, >, or =.

6. $\frac{2}{5}$ ◯ ⁻0.4

7. $\frac{^-3}{5}$ ◯ $\frac{^-4}{5}$

8. $\frac{3}{10}$ ◯ 0.5

9. $\frac{^-5}{5}$ ◯ ⁻1

10. ⁻0.25 ◯ $\frac{^-1}{5}$

11. 0.75 ◯ $\frac{^-4}{5}$

12. $\frac{3}{4}$ ◯ 0.5

13. $\frac{^-1}{4}$ ◯ ⁻0.25

14. **Stretch Your Thinking** Judy recorded the temperature at the same time on Monday, Tuesday, and Wednesday. The temperatures she recorded were $^-2\frac{1}{2}$°F, ⁻2.3°F, and $^-2\frac{2}{5}$°F. Wednesday's temperature was colder than Tuesday's, but warmer than Monday's. What was the temperature on each day?

_____

Homework

**Plan a trip stopping at the five cities shown on the map
(or choose and label five cities of your own).**

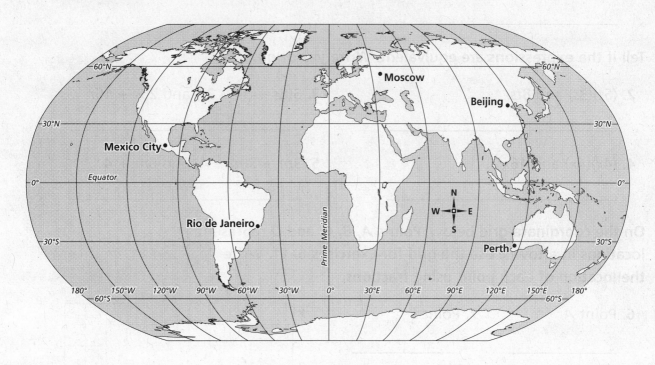

**Using + and − coordinates, write an ordered pair
to represent the approximate location of each city.**

1. Mexico City _____   **2.** Moscow _____

3. Perth _____   **4.** Rio de Janeiro _____

5. Beijing _____

6. Plan your route. Which city will you visit first? Second? And so on.

_____

_____

7. Use a map of the world or globe (or use the Internet with
a parent's or teacher's permission). Find or estimate the
distance between the cities on your route. Then estimate
the total distance of your trip. Is the total distance greater
than the distance around Earth (about 25,000 miles)?

_____

_____

Remembering

1. It costs $15.50 to buy 8 yards of material. How much does it cost to buy 20 yards of the same material?

_____

Tell if the expressions are equivalent. Write *yes* or *no*.

2. $(5t)(3s)$ and $8ts$

_____

3. $5(8s + 3r - 3s)$ and $25s + 15r$

_____

4. $(4x)(4x)$ and $16x^2$

_____

5. $3m + 3(m + 4)$ and $6m + 4$

_____

On the coordinate grid below, Points *A*, *B*, *C*, and *D* represent locations in a town. Use the grid for Exercises 6–11. Write the location of each point using fractions.

6. Point *A*

_____

7. Point *B*

_____

8. Point *C*

_____

9. Point *D*

_____

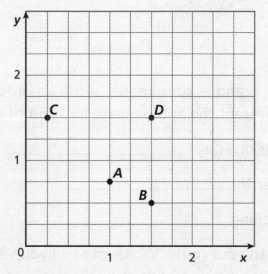

10. How far is Point *B* from Point *D*?

_____

11. How far is Point *C* from Point *D*?

_____

12. Stretch Your Thinking Suppose $(-2\frac{1}{2}, 1\frac{2}{5})$ was first reflected across the *y*-axis and then across the *x*-axis. What would be the new location and quadrant of the point? Explain.

_____

_____

_____

_____

Focus on Mathematical Practices